AN INDIAN PILGRIM

AUTOBIOGRAPHY OF SUBHAS CHANDRA BOSE

AN INDIAN PILGRIM

AUTOBIOGRAPHY OF SUBHAS CHANDRA BOSE

SUBHAS CHANDRA BOSE

GYAN

Published by

Gyan Publishing House
5, Ansari Road
Daryaganj, New Delhi-110002
Phone: 011-47034999, 9811692060
E-mail: books@gyanbooks.com

Distribution Network
gyanbooks.com
India, USA, Canada, UK, Australia

ISBN: 978-93-7316-041-2 (HB)

First Published, 1948

2nd Impression 2025

Printed at: Gyan Press, Delhi.

AN INDIAN PILGRIM
Author: SUBHAS CHANDRA BOSE

AN INDIAN PILGRIM

AUTOBIOGRAPHY OF SUBHAS CHANDRA BOSE

PUBLISHED FOR
NETAJI PUBLICATION SOCIETY
BY
THACKER, SPINK & CO. (1933) LTD.
CALCUTTA.
1948

PREFACE

The Netaji Publishing Society has great pleasure in presenting to the public the unfinished autobiography of Netaji Subhas Chandra Bose. Netaji wanted to give his autobiography, when completed, the title "An Indian Pilgrim". That is how his autobiography derives the name.

"An Indian Pilgrim" takes the reader from Netaji's parentage, birth and early childhood to his Cambridge days—and what days!—when a youngman of 24 had to make up his mind either to take a path, strewn with roses, which promised nothing but ease, luxury and official honour, or a path, strewn with thorns, inviting one to selfless suffering and sacrifice and promising nothing more than "blood, sweat and tears." The result of the struggle is known to the world. But only handful have had the privilege to know the different phases of that struggle. Perhaps it was not in 1921 but a decade earlier that the battle within had been won and lost. Perhaps even earlier! That is a poser which we leave to the readers. But one thing is certain that the Rashtrapati and the Rebel President, the Desh Gaurab and the Netaji, the creator of the First Government of the Free India and the beloved leader of the Hindus, Muslims, Sikhs, Christians and Parsees, had been moulded between 1897 and 1921. This is the period covered by "An Indian Pilgrim". It is the masterly analysis of a Humanitarian, a Psychologist, a Statesman and a Soldier, looking back on the formative years of his life.

It is the earnest desire of the Netaji Publishing Society to place before the public all the writings and speeches, political and autobiographical, of Netaji. A perusal of the yet unpublished materials at present at its disposal makes one's head whirl. One is forced into deeper thoughts at every step. The various facets of the struggle between the spiritual urge or the 'call of the Himalayas' and the cause of the suffering humanity; the nature of dreams Netaji used to have and their analysis by him and various other things make fascinating reading indeed, and they shall be made available to the public at the earliest opportunity. But many letters, articles, etc. written by Netaji are in the hands of the public. We would appeal to all to place them at the disposal of the Netaji Publishing Society so that they may run a thread through the scattered gems and return them to the world in the form of the most priceless ornament. We hope that all those who possess such materials shall rise above personal and private motives.

In conclusion, we would like to thank Shri Sudhir Chandra Roy Chowdhury (Mayor of Calcutta), Shri J. P. Mitter, Bar-at-Law, Shri Naresh Nath Mukherjee, Mr. M. V. Gough-Govia (Deputy Mayor) and Shri Madhusudan Dey of Messrs Thacker, Spink & Co., Ltd., for their kind assistance.

NETAJI ZINDABAD! JAI HIND!

SHAH NAWAZ KHAN.
SARDUL SINGH CAVEESHAR.
LAKSHMI SEHGAL.
MAHBOOB AHMED.
DHANRAJ SHARMA.
BIRENDRA N. DUTT.
BELA MITRA.
KALYAN KUMAR BOSE.

Calcutta, 23rd *January*, 1948.

CONTENTS

ILLUSTRATIONS

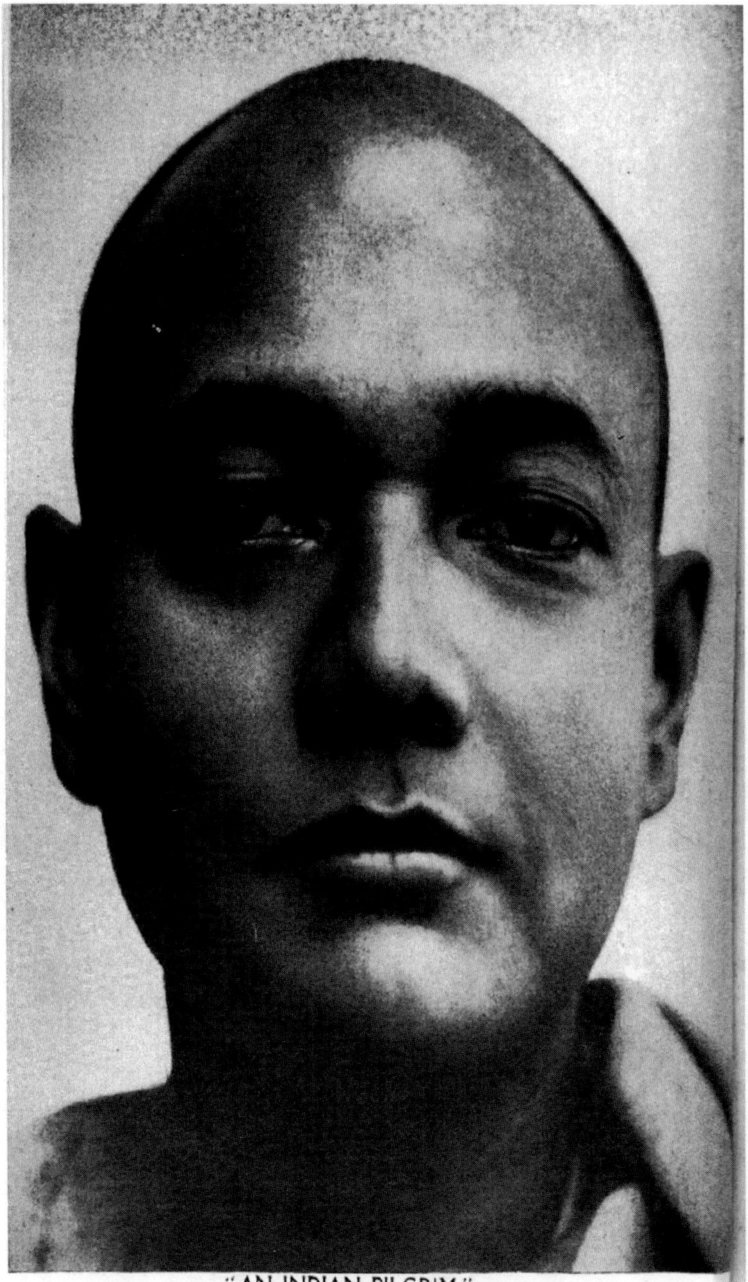

"AN INDIAN PILGRIM"
In Quest of India's Independence

CHAPTER ONE

BIRTH, PARENTAGE AND EARLY ENVIRONMENT

My father, Janakinath Bose, had migrated to Orissa in the eighties of the last century and had settled down at Cuttack as a lawyer. There I was born on Saturday, the 23rd January, 1897. My father was descended from the Boses of Mahinagar, while my mother, Prabhabati (or rather Prabhavati) belonged to the family of the Dutts of Hatkhola. I was the sixth son and the ninth child of my parents.

In these days of rapid communication, a night's journey by train southwards along the eastern coast takes one from Calcutta to Cuttack and on the way there is neither adventure nor romance. But things were not quite the same sixty years ago. One had to go either by cart and encounter thieves and robbers on the road, or by sea and brave the wrath of the winds and the waves. Since it was safer to trust in God than in brother man, it was more common to travel by boat. Sea-going vessels would carry passengers up to Chandbali where transhipment would take place and from Chandbali steamers would get to Cuttack through a number of rivers and canals. The description I used to hear from my mother since childhood of the rolling and pitching and the accompanying discomfort during the voyage would leave no desire in me to undergo such an experience. At a time when distances were long and journey by no means safe, my father must have had plenty of pluck to leave his village home and go far away in search of a career. Fortune favours the brave even in civil life and, by the time I was born, my father had already made a position for himself and was almost at the top of the legal profession in his new domicile.

Though a comparatively small town with a population in the neighbourhood of 20,000, Cuttack[1] had an importance of its own owing to a variety of factors. It had an unbroken tradition since the days of the early Hindu Kings of Kalinga. It was *de facto* capital of Orissa which could boast of such a famous place of pilgrimage as Puri (or Jagannath) and such glorious art-relics as those of Konarak, Bhuvaneswar, and Udaigiri. It was the headquarters not only for the British administration in Orissa, but also for the numerous ruling chiefs in that province. Altogether, Cuttack afforded a healthy environment for a growing child, and it had some of the virtues of both city and country life.

Ours was not a rich, but what might be regarded as a well-to-do, middle-class family. Naturally, I had no personal experience of what want and poverty meant and had no occasion to develop those traits of selfishness, greed, and the rest which are sometimes the unwelcome heritage of indigent circumstances in one's early life. At the same time, there was not that luxury and lavishness in our home which has been the ruin of so many promising but pampered young souls or has helped to foster a supercilious, high-brow mentality in them. In fact, considering their worldly means, my parents always

[1] Cuttack, under the Government of India Act, 1935, is the capital of the new province of Orissa. Formerly, till 1905, along with Bihar, it was a part of the Presidency of Bengal. Between 1905 and 1911 when Bengal was partitioned, West Bengal, Bihar and Orissa formed one province, while East Bengal and Assam formed another. After 1911 and till quite recently, Bihar and Orissa together formed one province. West and East Bengal have, since 1911, been re-united, while Assam and the Bengali speaking districts of Sylhet and Cachar have been constituted into a separate province.

erred—and, I daresay, rightly too—on the side of simplicity in the upbringing of their children.

The earliest recollection I have of myself is that I used to feel like a thoroughly insignificant being. My parents awed me to a degree. My father usually had a cloak of reserve round him and kept his children at a distance. What with his professional work and what with his public duties, he did not have much time for his family. The time he could spare was naturally divided among his numerous sons and daughters. The youngest child did, of course, come in for an extra dose of fondling, but an addition to the family would soon rob it of its title to special favour. And for the grown-ups it was difficult to discern whom father loved more, so strictly impartial he appeared to be, whatever his inner feelings might have been. And my mother? Though she was more humane and it was not impossible at times to detect her bias, she was also held in awe by most of her children. No doubt she ruled the roost and, where family affairs were concerned, hers was usually the last word. She had a strong will, and, when one added to that a keen sense of reality and sound common-sense, it is easy to understand how she could dominate the domestic scene. In spite of all the respect I cherished for my parents since my early years, I did yearn for a more intimate contact with them and could not help envying those children who were lucky enough to be on friendly terms with their parents. This desire presumably arose out of a sensitive and emotional temperament.

But to be overawed by my parents was not the only tragedy. The presence of so many elder brothers and sisters seemed to relegate me into utter insignificance. That was perhaps all to the good. I started life with a sense of diffidence—with a feeling that I should live up to the level already attained by those who had preceded me. For good or for ill, I was free from over-confidence or cocksureness. I lacked innate genius but had no tendency to shirk hard work. I had, I believe, a subconscious feeling that for mediocre men industry and good behaviour are the sole passports to success.

To be a member of a large family is, in many ways, a drawback. One does not get the individual attention which is often necessary in childhood. Moreover, one is lost in a crowd as it were, and the growth of personality suffers in consequence. On the other hand, one develops sociability and overcomes self-centredness and angularity. From infancy I was accustomed to living not merely in the midst of a large number of sisters and brothers, but also with uncles and cousins. The denotation of the word 'family' was therefore automatically enlarged. What is more, our house had always an open door for distant relatives hailing from our ancestral village. And, in accordance with a long-standing Indian custom, any visitors to the town of Cuttack who bore the stamp of respectability could—with or without an introduction—drive to our house and expect to be put up there. Where the hotel-system is not so much in vogue and decent hotels are lacking, society has somehow to provide for a social need.

The largeness of our household was due not merely to the size of the family, but to the number of dependants and servants as well—and to the representatives of the animal world—cows, horses, goats, sheep, deer, peacock, birds, mongoose, etc. The servants were an institution by themselves and formed an integral part of the household. Most of them had been in service long before I was born and some of them (e.g. the oldest maid-servant) were held in respect by all of us.[1] Commercialism had not then permeated and distorted human relationship; so there was considerable attachment between our servants and ourselves. This early experience shaped my subsequent mental attitude towards servants as a class.

Though the family environment naturally helped to broaden my mind, it could not, nevertheless, rid me of that shy reserve which was to haunt me for years later and which I doubt if I have yet been able to shake off. Perhaps I was and still remain an introvert.

[1] Some of them have since retired from service and are enjoying pensions, while others have died.

CHAPTER TWO

FAMILY HISTORY[1]

The history of our family can be traced back for about 27 generations. The Boses[2] are Kayastha[3] by caste. The founder of the Dakshin-Rarhi[4] clan of the Boses was one Dasaratha Bose, who had two sons, Krishna and Parama. Parama went over to East Bengal and settled there, while Krishna lived in West Bengal. One of the great-great-grandsons of Dasaratha was Mukti Bose, who resided at Mahinagar, a village about 14 miles to the south of Calcutta, whence the family is now known as the Boses of Mahinagar.[5] Eleventh in descent from Dasaratha was Mahipati, a man of outstanding ability and intelligence. He attracted the attention of the then King of Bengal, who appointed him as Minister for Finance and War. In appreciation of his services, the King, who was Muslim by religion, conferred on him the title of 'Subuddhi Khan'.[6] As was the prevailing custom, Mahipati was also given a 'jaigir' (landed property) as

[1] For some of the facts chronicled here I am indebted to Nagendranath Bose, the well-known antiquarian and historian (see his article on Purandar Khan in *Kayastha Patrika*, Bengali Monthly for Jaistha, 1885).

[2] The original form in Sanskrit is Basu or rather Vasu. In common parlance in Bengali, Vasu has become Bose.

[3] The Kayasthas claim to be none other than Kshatriyas (*i.e.*, warrior-caste) in origin. According to popular usage, the Kayasthas are classified among the (so-called) higher castes.

[4] Dakshin-Rarhi probably means 'South-Bengal'.

[5] From Calcutta Mahinagar can be reached *via* Chingripota, a station on the Diamond Harbour Railway line.

[6] It is interesting to note in this connection that the Muslim Kings of Bengal used Sanskrit words in their titles. 'Khan' is of course a typically Muslim title.

JANAKINATH WITH HIS FAMILY (Subhas Chandra on extreme right)

MOTHER
Inspirer of Religious Fervour

a mark of royal favour and the village of Subuddhipur, not far from Mahinagar, was probably his jaigir. Of Mahipati's ten sons, Ishan Khan, who was the fourth, rose to eminence and maintained his father's position at the Royal Court. Ishan Khan had three sons, all of whom received titles from the King. The second son, Gopinath Bose, possessed extraordinary ability and prowess and was appointed Finance Minister and Naval Commander by the then King, Sultan Hossain Shah (1493-1519). He was rewarded with the title of Purandar Khan and a jaigir, now known as Purandarpur, not far from his native village of Mahinagar. In Purandarpur there is a tank called "Khan Pukur" (or Khan's Tank) which is a relic of a one-mile long tank excavated by Purandar Khan. The village of Malancha near Mahinagar has grown on the site of Purandar's Garden.

In those days the Hooghly flowed in the vicinity of Mahinagar and it is said that Purandar used to travel by boat to and from Gaud, the then capital of Bengal. He built up a powerful navy which defended the kingdom from external attack and was its commander.

Purandar also made his mark as a social reformer. Before his time, according to the prevailing Ballali custom, the two wings of the Kayasthas—Kulin (who were the elite, viz., the Boses, the Ghoses, and the Mitras) and Moulik (the Dutts, the Deys, the Roys etc.) —did not, as a rule, intermarry. Purandar laid down a new custom[1] to the effect that only the eldest issue of

[1] Intercaste marriage which has been going on for the last 50 years or more has considerably slackened existing caste rules. But in Purandar's time this move was regarded as revolutionary. The outstanding position he had in social and public life enabled him to put through this measure of reform. It is said that he invited over 100,000 Kayasthas to his village to have the new code adopted by them. 'Khan's Pukur' was excavated on this occasion to supply pure drinking water to this vast assembly.

a Kulin need marry into a Kulin family, while the others could marry Mouliks. This custom, which has been generally followed till the present day, saved the Kayasthas from impending disaster—the fruit of excessive inbreeding.

Purandar was also a man of letters. His name figures among the composers of Padabali, the devotional songs of the Vaishnavas.

Evidence is afforded by several Bengali poems, like Kavirama's 'Raymangal', that as late as 200 years ago, the Hooghly (called in Bengali—Ganga) flowed by Mahinagar and the neighbouring villages. (Even now, all tanks in the former bed of the 'Ganga' are also called 'Ganga' by courtesy, e.g., Bose's Ganga, meaning thereby Bose's tank.) The shifting of the river-bed struck a death blow at the health and prosperity of these villages. Disturbance of the drainage of the countryside was followed by epidemics, which in turn forced a large section of the population to migrate to other places. One branch of the Bose family—the direct descendants of Purandar Khan—moved to the adjoining village of Kodalia.

After a period of comparative silence, this neighbourhood, containing the villages of Kodalia, Chingripota, Harinavi, Malancha, Rajpur, etc. leapt into activity once again. During the early decades of the nineteenth century there was a remarkable cultural upheaval which continued till the end of the century when once again the countryside was devastated by epidemics—malaria carrying off the palm this time. Today one has only to walk through these desolated villages and observe huge mansions overgrown with wild creepers standing in a dilapidated condition, in order to realise the degree of prosperity and culture which the neighbourhood must have enjoyed in the not distant past. The scholars who appeared here about a century ago were mostly men learned in the ancient lore of India, but they were not obscurantists by any means. Some of these Pundits were preceptors of the Brahmo Samaj, then a revolutionary body from the socio-cultural point of view, while others were editors of secular journals printed in Bengali which were playing an important part in creating a new Bengali literature and in influencing contemporary public affairs.

Pundit Ananda Chandra Vedantavageesh was the editor of *Tattwabodhini Patrika*, an influential journal of those days and also a preceptor of the Brahmo Samaj. Pundit Dwarakanath Vidyabhusan was the editor of *Som Prakash*, probably the first weekly journal to be printed in the Bengali language. One of his nephews was Pundit Shivanath Shastri, one of the outstanding personalities of the Brahmo Samaj. Bharat Chandra Shiromani was one of the authorities in Hindu Law, especially in the Bengal school of Hindu Law called 'Dayabhag'. Among the artists could be named Kalikumar Chakravarti, a distinguished painter, and among musicians, Aghor Chakravarti and Kaliprasanna Bose. During the last few decades the locality has played an important part in the nationalist movement. Influential Congressmen like Harikumar Chakravarti and Satkari Bannerji (who died in the Deoli Detention Camp in 1936) hail from this quarter, and no less a man than Comrade M. N. Roy, of international fame, was born there.

To come back to our story, the Boses who migrated to Kodalia must have been living there for at least ten generations, for their genealogical tree is available.[1] My father was the thirteenth in descent from Purandar

[1] See Appendix I.

Khan and twenty-sixth from Dasaratha Bose. My grandfather Haranath had four sons, Jadunath, Kedarnath, Devendranath, and Janakinath my father.

Though by tradition our family was Shakta,[1] Haranath was a pious and devoted Vaishnava. The Vaishnavas being generally more non-violent in temperament, Haranath stopped the practice of goat-sacrifice at the annual Durga Pooja (worship of God as Divine Energy in the form of mother) which used to be celebrated with great pomp every year—Durga Poojah being the most important festival of the Hindus of Bengal. This innovation has been honoured till the present day, though another branch of the Bose family living in the same village still adheres to goat-sacrifice at the annual Poojah.

Haranath's four sons migrated to different places in search of a career. The eldest Jadunath who worked in the Imperial Secretariat had to spend a good portion of his time in Simla. The second, Kedarnath, moved to Calcutta permanently. The third, Devendranath, who joined the educational service of the Government and rose to the rank of Principal, had to move about from place to place and after retirement settled down in Calcutta.

My father was born on the 28th May, 1860 and my mother in 1869.[2] After passing the Matriculation

[1] The Hindus of Bengal were, broadly speaking, divided into two schools or sects, Shakta and Vaishnava. Shaktas preferred to worship God as Power or Energy in the form of Mother. The Vaishnavas worshipped God as Love in the form of father and protector. The difference became manifest at the time of initiation, the 'mantra' or 'holy word' which a Shakta received from his 'guru', or preceptor, being different from what a Vaishnava received from his guru. It was customary for a family to follow a particular tradition for generations, though there was nothing to prevent a change from one sect to the other.

[2] To be more exact, she was born on the 13th Phalgun, 1275—according to the Bengali year. Phalgun 13th, 1344 is equivalent to February 25th, 1938.

(then called Entrance) Examination from the Albert School, Calcutta, he studied for some time at the St. Xavier's College and the General Assembly's Institution (now called Scottish Church College). He then went to Cuttack and graduated from the Ravenshaw College. He returned to Calcutta to take his law degree and during this period came into close contact with the prominent personalities of the Brahmo Samaj, Brahmanand Keshav Chandra Sen, his brother Krishna Vihari Sen, and Umesh Chandra Dutt, Principal of the City College. He worked for a time as Lecturer in the Albert College, of which Krishna Vihari Sen was the Rector. In 1885 he went to Cuttack and joined the bar. The year 1901 saw him as the first non-official elected Chairman of the Cuttack Municipality. By 1905 he became Government Pleader and Public Prosecutor. In 1912 he became a member of the Bengal Legislative Council and received the title of Rai Bahadur. In 1917, following some differences with the District Magistrate, he resigned the post of Government Pleader and Public Prosecutor and thirteen years later, in 1930, he gave up the title of Rai Bahadur as a protest against the repressive policy of the Government.

Besides being connected with public bodies like the Municipality and District Board, he took an active part in educational and social institutions like the Victoria School and Cuttack Union Club. He had extensive charities, and poor students came in for a regular share of them. Though the major portion of his charities went to Orissa, he did not forget his ancestral village, where he founded a charitable dispensary and library, named after his mother and father respectively. He was a regular visitor at the annual session of the Indian National Congress but he did not actively participate in politics, though he was a consistent supporter of Swadeshi.[1] After the commencement of the Non-co-operation Movement in 1921, he interested himself in the constructive activities of the Congress, Khadi[2] and national education. He was all along of a religious bent of mind and received initiation twice, his first guru being a Shakta and the second a Vaishnava. For years he was the President of the local Theosophical Lodge. He had always a soft spot for the poorest of the poor and before his death he made provisions for his old servants and other dependants.

As mentioned in the first chapter, my mother belonged to the family of the Dutts[3] of Hatkhola, a northern quarter of Calcutta. In the early days of British rule, the Dutts were one of those families in Calcutta who attained a great deal of prominence by virtue of their wealth and their ability to adapt themselves to the new political order. As a consequence, they played a rôle among the neo-aristocracy of the day. My mother's grandfather, Kashi Nath Dutt, broke away from the family and moved to Baranagore, a small town about six miles to the north of Calcutta, built a palatial house for himself and settled down there. He was a very well-educated man, a voracious reader and a friend of the students. He held a high administrative post in the firm of Messrs Jardine, Skinner & Co., a British firm doing business in Calcutta. Both my mother's father, Ganganarayan Dutt, and grandfather had a reputation for being wise in selecting their sons-in-law. They were thereby able to make alliances with

[1] *i.e.* home-industries.

[2] Khadi or Khaddar is hand-spun and hand-woven cloth.

[3] The original Sanskrit form of this word is "Datta" or "Dutta". "Dutt" is an anglicised abbreviation of this word.

the leading families among the Calcutta aristocracy of the day. One of Kashi Nath Dutt's sons-in-law was Sir Romesh Chandra Mitter,[1] who was the first Indian to be acting Chief Justice of the Calcutta High Court. Another was Rai Bahadur Hari Vallabh Bose who had migrated to Cuttack before my father and as a lawyer had won a unique position for himself throughout the whole of Orissa.

It is said of my maternal grandfather, Ganganarayan Dutt, that before he agreed to give my mother in marriage to my father, he put the latter through an examination and satisfied himself as to his intellectual ability. My mother was the eldest daughter. Her younger sisters were married successively to (the late) Barada Ch. Mitra, C.S., District and Sessions Judge, Mr Upendra Nath Bose of Benares City, (the late) Chandra Nath Ghose, Subordinate Judge and (the late) Dr J. N. Bose, younger brother of the late Rai Bahadur Chuni Lal Bose of Calcutta.

From the point of view of eugenics it is interesting to note that, on my father's side, large families were the exception and not the rule. On my mother's side, the contrary seems to have been the case. Thus my maternal grandfather had nine sons and six daughters.[2] Among his children, the daughters generally had large families—including my mother—but not the sons. My parents had eight sons and six daughters,[3] of whom nine—seven sons and two daughters—are still living.

[1] This is the same as Mitra. Sir Romesh had three sons—the late Manmatha Nath, Sir Benode, and Sir Pravas Mitter. The late Sir B. C. Mitter was Advocate-General of Bengal and later on, member of the Judicial Committee of the Privy Council. Sir Pravas Mitter was member of the Executive Council of the Governor of Bengal.

[2] For the genealogical tree, see Appendix II.

[3] See Appendix I.

Among my sisters and brothers, some—but not the majority—have as many as eight or nine children, but it is not possible to say that the sisters are more prolific than the brothers or *vice versa*. It would be interesting to know if in a particular family the prolific strain adheres to one sex more than to the other. Perhaps eugenists could answer the question.

CHAPTER THREE

BEFORE MY TIME

It requires a great deal of imagination now to picture the transformation that Indian Society underwent as a result of political power passing into the hands of the British since the latter half of the eighteenth century. Yet an understanding of it is essential if we are to view in their proper perspective the kaleidoscopic changes that are going on in India today. Since Bengal was the first province to come under British rule, the resulting changes were more quickly visible there than elsewhere. With the overthrow of the indigenous Government, the feudal aristocracy which was bound up with it naturally lost its importance. Its place was taken by another set of men. The Britishers had come into the country for purposes of trade and had later on found themselves called upon to rule. But it was not possible for a handful of them to carry on either trade or administration without the active co-operation of at least a section of the people. At this juncture those who fell in line with the new political order and had sufficient ability and initiative to make the most of the new situation came to the fore as the aristocracy of the new age.

It is generally thought that for a long time under British rule Muslims[1] did not play an important rôle, and several theories have been advanced to account for this. It is urged, for instance, that since, in provinces like Bengal, the rulers who were overthrown by the British were Muslims by religion, the Muslim community

[1] Also called Mohammedans.

maintained for a long time an attitude of sullen animosity and non-co-operation towards the new rulers, their culture and their administration. On the other hand it is said that, prior to the establishment of British rule in India, the Muslim aristocracy had already grown thoroughly effete and worn out and that Islam did not at first take kindly to modern science and civilization. Consequently, it was but natural that under British rule the Muslims should suffer from a serious handicap and go under for the time being. I am inclined, however, to think that in proportion to their numbers[1], and considering India as a whole, the Muslims have never ceased to play an important rôle in the public life of the country, whether before or under British rule—and that the distinction between Hindu and Muslim of which we hear so much nowadays is largely an artificial creation, a kind of Catholic-Protestant controversy in Ireland, in which our present-day rulers have had a hand. History will bear me out when I say that it is a misnomer to talk of Muslim rule when describing the political order in India prior to the advent of the British. Whether we talk of the Moghul Emperors at Delhi, or of the Muslim Kings of Bengal, we shall find that in either case the administration was run by Hindus and Muslims together, many of the prominent Cabinet Ministers and Generals being Hindus. Further, the consolidation of the Moghul Empire in India was effected with the help of Hindu commanders-in-chief. The commander-in-chief of Nawab Sirajudowla, whom the British fought at Plassey in 1757 and defeated, was a Hindu, and the

[1] According to the 1931 census, the Muslims are roughly 24.7 per cent of the total population of British India which is about 271.4 millions; roughly 13.5 per cent of the total population of the Indian states which is 79 millions and roughly 22 per cent of the total population of India, which is 350.5 millions.

rebellion of 1857 against the British, in which Hindus and Moslems were found side by side, was fought under the flag of a Muslim, Bahadur Shah.

Be that as it may, it is a fact so far as Bengal is concerned, whatever the causes may be, most of the prominent personalities that arose soon after the British conquest were Hindus. The most outstanding of them was Raja Ram Mohon Roy (1772-1833) who founded the Brahmo Samaj[1] in 1828. The dawn of the nineteenth century saw a new awakening in the land. This awakening was cultural and religious in character and the Brahmo Samaj was its spearhead. It could be likened to a combination of the Renaissance and Reformation. One aspect of it was national and conservative—standing for a revival of India's culture and a reform of India's religions. The other aspect of it was cosmopolitan and eclectic—seeking to assimilate what was good and useful in other cultures and religions. Ram Mohon was the visible embodiment of the new awakening and the herald of a new era in India's history. His mantle fell successively on 'Maharshi' Devendranath Tagore (1818-1905), father of the poet Rabindra Nath Tagore, and Brahmanand Keshav Chandra Sen (1838-1884) and the influence of the Brahmo Samaj grew from day to day.

There is no doubt that at one time the Brahmo Samaj focussed within itself all the progressive movements and tendencies in the country. From the very beginning the Samaj was influenced in its cultural

[1] The Brahmo Samaj can best be described as a reformist movement within Hindu society, standing for the religious principles of the Vedanta in their pristine form and discarding later accretions like image-worship and the caste-system. Originally the Brahmos tended to break away from Hindu society, but their present attitude is to regard themselves as an integral part of it.

outlook by Western science and thought, and when the newly established British Government was in doubt as to what its educational policy should be—whether it should promote indigenous culture exclusively or introduce Western culture—Raja Ram Mohon Roy took an unequivocal stand as the champion of Western culture. His ideas influenced Thomas Babington Macaulay when he wrote his famous Minute on Education[1] and ultimately became the policy of the Government. With his prophetic vision, Ram Mohon had realised, long before any of his countrymen did, that India would have to assimilate Western science and thought if she wanted to come into her own once again.

The cultural awakening was not confined to the Brahmo Samaj, however. Even those who regarded the Brahmos as too heretical, revolutionary, or iconoclastic were keen about the revival of the indigenous culture of India. While the Brahmos and other progressive sections of the people replied to the challenge of the West by trying to assimilate all that was good in Western culture, the more orthodox circles responded by justifying whatever there was to be found in Hindu society and by trying to prove that all the discoveries and inventions of the West were known to the ancient sages of India. Thus the impact of the West roused even the orthodox circles from their self-complacency. There was a great deal of literary activity among them and they produced able men like Sasadhar Tarkachuramani—but much of their energy was directed towards

[1] Macaulay came to Calcutta as Law Member of the Governor General's Council in the autumn of 1834. He was appointed President of the Committee of Public Instruction which he found divided into the Orientalist and English parties. On February 2, 1835, he submitted a Minute to the Governor General, Bentinck, supporting the English party which was adopted by the Government.

meeting the terrible onslaughts on Hindu religion coming from the Christian missionaries. In this there was common ground between the Brahmos and the orthodox Pundits, though in other matters there was no love lost between them. Out of the conflict between the old and the new, between the conservatives and the radicals, between the Brahmos and the Pundits, there emerged a new type—the noblest embodiment of which was Pundit Iswar Chandra Vidyasagar. This new type of Indian stood for progress and for a synthesis of Eastern and Western culture and accepted generally the spirit of reform which was abroad, but refused to break away from Hindu society or to go too far in emulating the West, as the Brahmos were inclined to do at first. Iswar Chandra Vidyasagar, for instance, was brought up as an orthodox Pundit, became the father of modern Bengali prose and a protagonist of Western science and culture, and was a great social reformer and philanthropist[1]—but till the last, he stuck to the simple and austere life of an orthodox Pundit. He boldly advocated the remarriage of Hindu widows and incurred the wrath of the conservatives in doing so—but he based his arguments mainly on the fact that the ancient scriptures approved of such a custom. The type which Iswar Chandra represented ultimately found its religious and philosophical expression in Ramakrishna Paramahansa (1834-1886) and his worthy disciple, Swami Vivekananda (1863-1902). Swami Vivekananda died in 1902 and the religio-philosophical movement was continued through the

[1] Speaking of the Pundit, the poet Madhusudan Dutt, the originator of blank verse in Bengali, once wrote—"You are not merely the ocean of knowledge (vidyasagar means literally 'the ocean of knowledge') as people know you in India, but also the ocean of generosity."

personality of Arabindo Ghose (or Ghosh). Arabindo did not keep aloof from politics. On the contrary, he plunged into the thick of it, and by 1908 became one of the foremost political leaders. In him, spirituality was wedded to politics. Arabindo retired from politics in 1909 to devote himself exclusively to religion; but spirituality and politics continued to be associated together in the life of Lokamanya B. G. Tilak (1856-1920) and Mahatma Gandhi (1869).

This brief narrative will serve as a rough background to the contents of this book and will give some idea of the social environment which existed when my father was a student of the Albert School[1] in Calcutta. Society was then dominated by a new aristocracy, which had grown up alongside of British rule, whom we should now call, in socialist parlance, the allies of British 'Imperialism. This aristocracy was composed roughly of three classes or professions—(1) landlords, (2) lawyers and civil servants and (3) merchant-princes. All of them were the creation of the British, their assistance being necessary for carrying out the policy of administration-cum-exploitation.

The landlords who came into prominence under British rule were not the semi-independent or autonomous chiefs of the feudal age, but mere tax-collectors who were useful to a foreign Government in the matter of collecting land-revenue and who had to be rewarded for their loyalty during the Rebellion of 1857, when the existence of British rule hung by a thread.

Though the new aristocracy dominated contemporary society and, as a consequence, men like Maharaja Jatindra Mohon Tagore and Raja Benoy Krishna Deb

[1] Here he was a class-fellow of Sir P. C. Ray, the well-known chemist and philanthropist.

Bahadur were regarded by the Government as the leaders of society, they had little in the way of intellectual or moral appeal. That appeal was exercised in my father's youth by men like Keshav Chandra Sen and to some extent, Iswar Chandra Vidyasagar. Wherever the former went, crowds followed him. He was, indeed, the hero of the hour. The spiritual fervour of his powerful orations raised the moral tone of society as a whole and of the rising generations in particular. Like other students, my father, too, came under his magic influence, and there was a time when he even thought of a formal conversion to Brahmoism. In any case, Keshav Chandra undoubtedly had an abiding influence on my father's life and character. Years later, in far-off Cuttack, portraits of this great man would still adorn the walls of his house, and his relations with the local Brahmo Samaj continued to be cordial throughout his life.

Though there was a profound moral awakening among the people during the formative period of my father's life, I am inclined to think that politically the country was still dead. It is significant that his heroes —Keshav Chandra and Iswar Chandra[1]—though they were men of the highest moral stature, were by no means anti-Government or anti-British. The former used to state openly that he regarded the advent of the British as a divine dispensation. And the latter did not shun contact with the Government or with Britishers as a 'non-co-operator' today would, though the keynote of his character was an acute sense of independence and

[1] Both of them were educationists and, largely under their inspiration, a new type of teachers, possessing a high moral character, was produced. My father was also a teacher for some time and might have taken up teaching as a profession.

self-respect. My father, likewise, though he had a high standard of morality, and influenced his family to that end, was not anti-Government. That was why he could accept the position of Government Pleader and Public Prosecutor, as well as a title from the Government. My father's elder brother, Principal Devendra Nath Bose, belonged to the same type. He was a man of unimpeachable character, greatly loved and respected by his students for his intellectual and moral attainments, but he was a Government servant in the Education Department. Likewise, before my father's time it was possible for Bankim Chandra Chatterji[1] (1838-1894) to compose the "Bande Mataram"[2] song and still continue in Government service. And D. L. Roy[3] could be a magistrate in the service of the Government and yet compose national songs which inspired the people. All this could happen some decades ago, because that was an age of transition, probably an age of political immaturity. Since 1905, when the partition of Bengal was effected in the teeth of popular opposition and indignation, a sharpening of political consciousness has taken place, leading to inevitable friction between the people and the Government. People are nowadays more resentful of what the Government does and the Government in its turn is more suspicious of what the people say or write. The old order has changed yielding place to new, and today it is no longer possible to separate morality from politics—to obey the dictates of morality and not land oneself in political trouble. The individual has to go through the experi-

[1] One of the fathers of modern Bengali Literature.

[2] 'Bande Mataram' literally means 'I salute the mother' (i.e. motherland). It is the nearest approach to India's national anthem.

[3] One of the foremost Bengali dramatists and composer of national songs—father of Dilip Kumar Roy. He died in 1913.

ence of his race within the brief span of his own life, and I remember quite clearly that I too passed through the stage of what I may call non-political morality, when I thought that moral development was possible while steering clear of politics—while complacently giving unto Caesar what is Caesar's. But now I am convinced that life is one whole. If we accept an idea, we have to give ourselves wholly to it and to allow it to transform our entire life. A light brought into a dark room will necessarily illuminate every portion of it.

CHAPTER FOUR

AT SCHOOL (1).

I was nearing my fifth birthday (January, 1902) when I was told I would be sent to school. I do not know how other children have felt in similar circumstances, but I was delighted. To see your elder brothers and sisters dress and go to school day after day and be left behind at home simply because you are not big enough—not old enough—is a galling experience. At least, so I had felt, and that is why I was overjoyed.

It was to be a red-letter day for me. At long last I was going to join the grown-up respectable folks who did not stay at home except on holidays. We had to start at about 10 a.m. because the classes commenced exactly at 10 a.m. Two uncles of about the same age as myself were also to be admitted along with myself. When we were all ready, we began to run towards the carriage which was to take us to school. Just then, as ill-luck would have it, I slipped and fell. I was hurt and, with a bandage round my head, I was ordered to bed. The rumbling of the carriage wheels grew fainter in the distance. The lucky ones had gone, but there I lay with darkness staring me in the face and my fond hopes dashed to the ground.

Twenty-four hours later I found solace.

Ours was a missionary school[1] meant primarily for European and Anglo-Indian boys and girls with a limited number of seats (about 15 per cent) for Indians. All our brothers and sisters had joined this school, and so I did. I do not know why our parents had selected

[1] Protestant European School (P. E. School) run by the Baptist Mission.

this school, but I presume it was because we would master the English language better and sooner there than elsewhere, and knowledge of English had a premium in those days. I still remember that when I went to school I had just learnt the English alphabet and no more. How I managed to get along without being able to speak a word of English beats me now. I have not yet forgotten one of my first attempts at English. We had been given slate pencils and told to sharpen them before trying to write. Mine was done better than that of my uncle; so I pointed that out to our teacher by saying, "Ranendra mot[1] I shor[2]"—and thought that I had talked in English.

Our teachers were Anglo-Indians (and mostly ladies) with the exception of the headmaster and headmistress, Mr and Mrs Young, who had come out from England. Most of our teachers we did not fancy. Some like Mr Young we feared, though we respected, for he was too liberal with his cane. Some like Miss Cadogan we tolerated. Others like Miss S. we positively hated and would cry 'Hurrah' if she ever absented herself. Mrs Young we liked, but Miss Sarah Lawrence who was our first teacher in the Infant Class we loved. She had such a sympathetic understanding of the child's mind that we were irresistibly drawn towards her. But for her, I doubt if I would have got on so easily at a time when I was unable to express myself in English.

Though the majority of the teachers and pupils were Anglo-Indians, the school was based on the English model and run on English lines, as far as Indian conditions would permit. There were certain things we did

[1] 'Mota' in Bengali means 'thick' and 'mot' was a distortion of it.
[2] 'Shoroo' in Bengali means 'thin' and 'shor' was a distortion of it.

learn there which we would have missed in an Indian school. There was not that unhealthy emphasis on studies which obtains in Indian schools. Outside studies, more attention was given to deportment, neatness, and punctuality than is done in an Indian school. In the matter of studies, the students received more individual attention at the hands of their teachers and the daily work was done more regularly and systematically than is possible in an Indian school. The result was that practically no preparation was needed when an examination had to be faced. Moreover, the standard of English taught was much higher than that of Indian schools. But after giving due consideration and credit to all this, I doubt if I should today advise an Indian boy to go to such a school. Though there was order and system in the education that was imparted, the education itself was hardly adapted to the needs of Indian students. Too much importance was attached to the teaching of the Bible, and the method of teaching it was as unscientific as it was uninteresting. We had to learn our Bible lessons by heart whether we understood anything or not, as if we were so many priests memorizing the sacred texts. It would be no exaggeration for me to say that though we were taught the Bible day in, day out, for seven long years, I came to like the Bible for the first time several years later when I was in College.

There is no doubt that the curriculum was so framed as to make us as English in our mental make-up as possible. We learnt much about the geography and history of Great Britain but proportionally little about India—and when we had to negotiate Indian names, we did so as if we were foreigners. We started our Latin declensions—'bonus, bona, bonum'—rather early and did not have to be bothered about our Sanskrit declensions—'Gajah, Gajow, Gajah'—till we had left the P. E. School. When it came to music, we had to train our ears to 'Do, Ray, Me, Fah' and not to 'Sah, Ray, Gah, Mah'. The readers contained stories and anecdotes from English history or fairy tales which are current in Europe and there was not a word in them of Indian origin. Needless to add, no Indian language was taught[1] and so we neglected our mother-tongue altogether until we joined an Indian School.

It would be wrong to conclude from the above that we were not happy at school. On the contrary. During the first few years we were not conscious at all that the education imparted was not suited to Indian conditions. We eagerly learnt whatever came our way and fell completely in line with the school-system, as the other pupils did. The school had a reputation for turning out well-behaved boys and girls, and we tried to live up to it. Our parents, I think, were on the whole satisfied with our progress. With the school-authorities our stock was high, because the members of our family were generally at the top in whichever class they happened to be.

Sports naturally came in for some amount of attention, but not as much as one would expect in a school run on English lines. That was probably due to the fact that our headmaster was not much of a sportsman himself. He was a unique personality in many ways and strong-willed—and the stamp of his character was visible everywhere within the precincts of the school. He was a stern disciplinarian and a great stickler for good behaviour. In the Progress Report marks were given not only for the different subjects but also for (1) Conduct, (2) Deportment, (3) Neatness,

[1] I believe there has been a change for the better in recent years.

(4) Punctuality. No wonder therefore that the boys and girls turned out were well-mannered. For misbehaviour or indiscipline, boys were liable to be flogged[1] with a cane, but only two of the teachers had this authority—the headmaster and his worthy spouse.

Mr Young had several idiosyncrasies, however, and many were the jokes we would have at his expense. He had an elder brother, a bachelor and a missionary with a venerable beard, who was exceedingly fond of children and would love to play with them. To distinguish our headmaster from his elder brother, we nicknamed him "Young Young", the latter being called "Old Young". Mr Young Young was very sensitive to cold and even on a warm day he would shut the windows lest the draught should come in. He would frequently warn us about the risk of catching cold and getting cholera therefrom. If he ever felt out of sorts, he would take such a stiff dose of quinine as would make him almost deaf. After he had lived twenty years in the country, he could speak hardly a word in the local dialect and never cared to go in for sight-seeing or touring. If the caretaker forgot to put something on his table, Mr Young would ring for him, point to the thing wanted, but, unable to scold him in the local dialect, would content himself with glaring at him and then muttering, "All this ought to have been done before". If a messenger brought in a letter and Mr Young wanted to ask him to wait, he would run up to his wife, get the correct words from her, and go on repeating them till he was able to come out and throw them at the man.

[1] Nobody seemed to mind the caning which Mrs Young administered, for the boys usually came smiling out of her room. But the headmaster's flogging was a different story altogether and there was hardly any boy who would not turn pale as he growled, "Go into my room, Sir".

With all this our headmaster was a man who bore himself with dignity and poise and commanded our respect, though it was tinged with fear. Our headmistress was a motherly lady who was universally liked. And I must say that there was never any attempt to influence unduly our social and religious ideas. Things went on smoothly for some years and we seemed to have fitted into our *milieu* splendidly, but gradually there appeared a rift within the lute. Something happened which tended to differentiate us from our environment. Was it the effect of local causes or was it the echo of larger socio-political disturbances; that is a poser I shall not answer for the present.

To some extent this differentiation was inevitable, but what was not inevitable was the conflict that arose out of it. We had been living in two distinct worlds and as our consciousness developed we began to realise slowly that these two worlds did not always match. There was, on the one hand, the influence of family and society which was India. There was, on the other, another world, another atmosphere, where we spent most of our working days, which was not England, of course, but a near approach to it. We were told that, because we were Indians, we could not sit for scholarship examinations[1], like Primary School and Middle School Examinations, though in our annual examinations many of us were topping the class. Anglo-Indian boys could join the Volunteer Corps and shoulder a rifle, but we could not. Small incidents like these began to open our eyes to the fact that as Indians we were a class apart, though we belonged to the same institution. Then there would be occasional quarrels between English (or Anglo-Indian) and Indian

[1] This was because Indian boys would carry away the scholarships.

boys which would finish up with a boxing bout[1], in which sympathies would be mobilized along racial lines. The son of a very high Indian official who was a fellow-student would organise matches between Indians and Europeans at his place, and those of us who could play well would join either side. I can also remember that we Indian boys talking among ourselves would sometimes say that we were fed up with the Bible and that for nothing in the world would we ever change our religion. Then there came the new regulations of the Calcutta University making Bengali a compulsory subject for the Matriculation, Intermediate and Degree Examinations and introducing other changes in the Matriculation curriculum. We were soon made to realise that the curriculum of the P. E. School did not suit us and that, unlike the other boys, we would have to begin anew the study of Bengali and Sanskrit when we joined an Indian school in order to prepare for the Matriculation Examination. Last but not least, there was the influence of my elder brothers who had already left our school and were preparing for the Matriculation, Intermediate and Degree Examinations and who spoke to us at home of a different world in which they moved about.

It would be wrong to infer from the above that I was in revolt against my school-environment after I had been there some years. I was there for seven years, from 1902 to 1908, and was to all intents and purposes satisfied with my surroundings. The disturbing factors referred to above were passing incidents which did not affect the even tenor of our life. Only towards the end did I have a vague feeling of unhappiness, of mal-

[1] In these bouts my uncles and some of my brothers always gave a good account of themselves.

adaptation[1] to my environment and a strong desire to join an Indian school where, so I thought, I would feel more at home. And strangely enough, when in January, 1909, I shook hands with our headmaster and said good-bye to the school, the teachers and the students, I did so without any regret, without a momentary pang. At the time, it was quite impossible for me to understand what had gone wrong with me. Only from this distance of time and with the help of an adult mind can I now analyse some of the factors that had been at work.

So far as studies were concerned my record during this period was satisfactory, because I was usually at the top. But as I did badly in sports and did not play any part in the bouts that took place, and as studies did not have the importance which they have usually in an Indian school, I came to cherish a poor opinion of myself.[2] The feeling of insignificance—of diffidence—to which I have referred before, continued to haunt me. Having joined the lowest standard I had probably got into the habit of looking up to others and of looking down upon myself.

Considering everything, I should not send an Indian boy or girl to such a school now. The child will certainly suffer from a sense of maladaptation and from consequent unhappiness, especially if he or she is of a sensitive nature. I should say the same of the practice of sending Indian boys to public schools in England which prevailed and still prevails[3] in certain aristocratic

[1] It is possible that this feeling grew within me because I was too much of an introvert, as I have remarked at the end of the first chapter.

[2] Perhaps this was responsible to some extent for the feeling of unhappiness to which I have referred in the preceding paragraph.

[3] I am fortified in this view by what I saw of the Indian products of English public schools when I was a student at Cambridge.

circles in India. For the same reason, I strongly condemn the move taken by certain Indians to start Indian schools run by English teachers on the lines of English public schools. It is possible that some boys, for example those who are mentally extrovert, may not suffer from a feeling of maladaptation and may feel quite happy in such an environment. But introvert children are bound to suffer, and in that event the reaction against the system and all that it stands for is bound to be hostile. Apart from this psychological consideration, a system of education which ignores Indian conditions, Indian requirements, and Indian history and sociology is too unscientific to commend itself to any rational support. The proper psychological approach for a cultural rapprochement between the East and the West is not to force 'English' education on Indian boys when they are young, but to bring them into close personal contact with the West when they are developed, so that they can judge for themselves what is good and what is bad in the East and in the West.

CHAPTER FIVE

AT SCHOOL (2)

It is strange how your opinion of yourself can bc influenced by what others think of you. In January, 1909, when I joined the Ravenshaw Collegiate School, Cuttack, a sudden change came over me. Among European and Anglo-Indian boys my parentage had counted for nothing, but among our own people it was different. Further, my knowledge of English was above the ordinary level and that gave me an added estimation in the eyes of my new class-mates. Even the teachers treated me with undue consideration, because they expected me to stand first, and in an Indian school studies, and not sports, brought credit and reward. At the first quarterly examination I did justify the hopes placed in me. The new atmosphere in which I lived and moved forced me to think better of myself—that I was worth something and was not an insignificant creature. It was not a feeling of pride that crept into me but of self-confidence, which till then had been lacking and which is the *sine qua non* of all success in life.

This time it was not the infant class which I joined but the fourth[1] class—so I did not have to look up all the time. Boys of the fourth class considered themselves as belonging to one of the higher classes and moved about with an air of importance. So did I. But in one respect I was seriously handicapped in spite of all the other advantages I enjoyed. I had read hardly a word of Bengali—my mother-tongue—before I joined

[1] In our time the numbering was different from what obtains now. For instance, formerly the first class was the top class in a High School.

this school, while the other boys had already reached a high standard. I remember that the first day I had to write an essay on 'Cow' (or was it 'Horse'?), I was made the laughing-stock of all my class-mates. I knew nothing of grammar and precious little of spelling and when the teacher read out my composition to the whole class with running comments, punctuated with laughter, flowing in from all sides, I felt humbled to the dust. I had never had this experience before—to be laughed at for deficiency in studies—and on top of it, I had lately developed a species of self-consciousness which had made me ultrasensitive. For weeks and months the Bengali lessons would give me the creeps. But for the time being, however acute the mental torture, there was nothing I could do but put up with the humiliation and secretly resolve to make good. Slowly and steadily I began to gain ground and at the annual examination I had the satisfaction of getting the highest marks in that subject.

I enjoyed my new surroundings, the more so as I had longed for the change. At the other school, though I had been there for seven years, I had not left behind any friends. Here it looked as if I would enter into lasting friendship with at least some of my class-mates. My friends were not of the sporting type because I did not take kindly to sports and only the drill lessons interested me. Apart from my own lukewarmness, there was another obstacle to my taking to sports enthusiastically. It was customary for the boys to return home after school-hours, have a light tiffin, and then go out for games. My parents did not like us to do that. Either they thought that sports would interfere with our studies or they did not regard the atmosphere of the playground as congenial to our mental health. Possibly the latter consideration weighed more with them. Be that as it may, the domestic situation was such that if we wanted to go out for games, we had to do it on the sly. Some of my brothers and uncles did do so and occasionally, when they were caught, were given a talking-to. But, knowing my parents' habits, it was generally possible to dodge them, especially as they were in the habit of going out for a drive and walk. If I had had a strong desire like the others, I could easily have joined them at the games. But I did not. Moreover, I was then of a goody-goody nature and was busy devouring ethical verses in Sanskrit. Some of these verses taught that the highest virtue consisted in obeying one's father—that when one's father was satisfied all the gods were satisfied[1]—that one's mother was even greater than one's father etc., etc. I therefore thought it better not to do what would displease my parents. So I would take to gardening along with those who did not go out for games. We had a fairly big kitchen and flower garden adjoining our house and in company with the gardener we would water and tend the plants or do some digging or help lay out the beds. Gardening I found absorbingly interesting. It served, among other things, to open my eyes to the beauties of nature, about which I shall have something to say later on. Besides gardening, we would also go in for physical exercise and gymnastics for which there were arrangements at home.

Looking back on my past life I feel inclined to think that I should not have neglected sports. By doing so, I probably developed precocity and accentuated my introvert tendencies. To ripen too early is not good, either for a tree or for a human being and

[1] Pitah Swargah, Pitah Dharmah, Pitahi Paramantapah etc.

one has to pay for it in the long run. There is nothing to beat nature's law of gradual development, and however much prodigies may interest us at first they generally fail to fulfil their early promise.

For two years life rolled on in much the same way. Among the teachers and students there were both Bengalees and Oriyas and the relations between them were quite cordial. One did not hear in those days—at least we students did not hear—of any ill-feeling or misunderstanding between the people of the two sister provinces. So far as the members of our family were concerned, we could never think or feel in terms of narrow parochialism or provincialism. For that we have to thank our parents. My father had extensive contacts with the people of Orissa, and intimate personal relations with many distinguished Oriya families. His outlook was consequently broad and his sympathies wide and they unconsciously influenced the rest of his family. I cannot remember ever to have heard from his lips one single disparaging remark about the people of Orissa—or for the matter of that about the people of any other province. Though he was never effusive in his emotions and was inclined to be reserved, he could endear himself to all those who came into contact with him wherever he happened to be at the time. Such parental influences work unobtrusively and only in later life can the children discover by a process of analysis what helped to mould their character or give their life a definite direction.

Of the teachers there was one who left a permanent impression on my youthful mind. That was our headmaster, Babu Beni Madhav Das. The very first day I saw him taking his rounds—and I was then just over twelve—I felt what I should now call an irresistible moral appeal in his personality. Up till then I had never experienced what it was to respect a man. But for me, to see Beni Madhav Das was to adore him. I was not old enough then to realise what it was that I adored. I could only feel that here was a man who was not an ordinary teacher, who stood apart from, and above, the rest of his tribe. And I secretly said to myself that if I wanted an ideal for my life, it should be to emulate him.

Talking of an ideal, I am reminded of an experience I had when I was at the P. E. School. I was then about ten. Our teacher asked us to write an essay on what we would like to be when we were grown-up. My eldest brother was in the habit of giving us talks on the respective virtues of a judge, magistrate, commissioner, barrister, doctor, engineer, and so forth, and I had picked up odd things from what I had heard him say. I jumbled up as many of these as I still remembered and wound up by saying that I would be a magistrate. The teacher remarked that to be a magistrate after being a commissioner would be an anti-climax, but I was too young to understand the status of the different professions and designations. After that I had no occasion to be worried by the thought of what I should aspire to be in later life. I only remember hearing in talks within the family circle that the highest position one could get to was the Indian Civil Service.[1]

The headmaster did not usually give any regular lessons till the boys reached the second class. So I began to long for the day when I would reach the second class and be entitled to listen to his lectures. That day did arrive,[2] but my good fortune did not last

[1] In those days it was nicknamed the heaven-born service.

[2] I was then fourteen.

long. After a few months orders for his transfer came. However, before he left us he had succeeded in rousing in me a vague perception of moral values—an inchoate feeling that in human life moral values should count more than anything else. In other words he had made me feel the truth of what we had read in our Poetry-Book—

"The rank is but the guinea's stamp
The man is the gold for all that."

And it was well that he had, for about this time the usual mental changes—best described in scientific terminology as sex-consciousness—which are incidental to approaching puberty, began to overtake me.

I remember vividly the parting scene when headmaster Beni Madhav took leave of his devoted and admiring pupils. He entered the class-room visibly moved and, in a voice ringing with emotion, said, "I have nothing more to say but invoke the blessings of God on you . . . . " I could not listen any more. Tears rushed to my eyes and I cried out within myself. But a hundred eyes were on the alert and I managed to restrain myself. The classes were then dismissed and the boys began to file off. Passing near his room I suddenly saw him standing in the verandah watching the boys depart. Our eyes met. The tears which I had managed to restrain within the class-room now began to flow. He saw them and was also moved. I stood paralysed for a moment and he came up to say that we would meet again. This was, I believe, the first time in my life that I had to weep at the time of parting and the first time I realised that only when we are forced to part do we discover how much we love.[1]

[1] I have had repeated demonstrations of this principle in later life.

The next day there was a public meeting organised by the staff and students to accord him a farewell. I was one of those who had to speak. How I got through my part I do not know, for internally I was all in tears. I was, however, painfully surprised to find that there were many among the staff and the students who did not realise at all what a sorrowful event it was. When the headmaster spoke in reply, his words seemed to pierce through my soul. I could hear only his opening words saying that he had never expected, when he first came to Cuttack, that there would be so much affection in store for him. Then I ceased to listen but continued to gaze at his impassioned countenance, which spoke volumes to me. There was an expression, a glow, therein—which I had seen in the portraits of Keshav Chandra Sen. And no wonder, since he was Keshav Chandra's ardent disciple and devotee.[1]

It was now a different school altogether—so dull, uninteresting, and uninspiring—for a light that had hitherto shone there had vanished. But there was no help, the classes had to be attended, the lessons learnt, and the examinations taken. The wheel of life grinds on regardless of our joys and sorrows.

It is interesting how you can sometimes come nearer to a person when you have parted from him. This happened in the present case. I started a correspondence with Headmaster Beni Madhav which went on for some years. One thing I now learnt from him—how to love nature and be inspired by her, not merely aesthetically, but ethically as well. Following his instructions, I took to what, in the absence of anything better, might be described as a species of nature-worship. I would choose a beauty-spot on the river-bank

[1] There is a saying in Sanskrit—"As you think, so you become".

or on a hill or in a lonely meadow in the midst of an enchanting sunset-glow, and practise contemplation. 'Surrender yourself completely to nature', he would write, 'and let nature speak to you through her Protean mask'. This sort of contemplation had given him peace of mind, joy, and strength of will.

How far I profited ethically from this effort I cannot say. But it certainly opened my eyes to the hidden and neglected beauties of nature and also helped me to concentrate my mind. In the garden, among flowers, sprouting leaves and growing plants, I would find an indescribable joy and I would love to ramble, alone or in the company of friends, amid the wild beauties of nature with which the countryside was so plentifully supplied. I could realise the truth of what the poet had said—

> "A primrose by the river's brim,
> A yellow primrose is to him,
> And it is something more."

Wordsworth's poems now had an added significance for me and I would simply revel in the descriptions of natural scenery in Kalidas's[1] poetry and in the Mahabharata[2] which, thanks to my Pundit, I could enjoy in the original Sanskrit.

I was at this time entering on one of the stormiest periods in my psychical life which was to last for five or six years. It was a period of acute mental conflict causing untold suffering and agony, which could not be shared by any friends and was not visible to any outsider. I doubt if a growing boy normally goes through

[1] The greatest poet and dramatist of ancient India who wrote in Sanskrit.

[2] The *Mahabharata* and *Ramayana* are the two greatest epics of ancient India.

this experience—at least I hope he does not. But I had in some respects a touch of the abnormal in my mental make-up. Not only was I too much of an introvert, but I was in some respects precocious. The result was that at an age when I should have been tiring myself out on the football field, I was brooding over problems which should rather have been left to a more mature age. The mental conflict, as I view it from this distance, was a two-fold one. Firstly, there was the natural attraction of a worldly life and of worldly pursuits in general, against which my higher self was beginning to revolt. Secondly, there was the growth of sex-consciousness, quite natural at that age, but which I considered unnatural and immoral and which I was struggling to suppress or transcend.

Nature-worship, as described above, was elevating and therefore helpful to a certain point, but it was not enough. What I required—and what I was unconsciously groping after—was a central principle, which I could use as a peg to hang my whole life on, and a firm resolve to have no other distractions in life. It was no easy job to discover this principle or idea and then consecrate my life to it. My agony could have been terminated, or at least considerably mitigated, if I had either given in at the outset as so many have done, or had with one bold effort of the will fixed on an idea and heroically brushed aside all other allurements. But I would not give in—there was something within which would not let me do so. I had therefore to fight on. And a stiff fight it was, because I was weak. For me the difficulty was not about the determination of life's goal so much as about concentrating my entire will to that single goal. Even after I had decided what was the most desirable object in life, it took me a long time to establish peace and harmony within myself by bringing under control contrary or rebellious tendencies, for though the spirit was willing the flesh was weak. A stronger will than mine would undoubtedly have managed things more easily.

One day by sheer accident I stumbled upon what turned out to be my greatest help in this crisis. A relative of mine,[1] who was a new-comer to the town, was living next door and I had to visit him. Glancing over his books, I came across the works of Swami Vivekananda. I had hardly turned over a few pages when I realised that here was something which I had been longing for. I borrowed the books from him, brought them home, and devoured them. I was thrilled to the marrow of my bones. My headmaster had roused my aesthetic and moral sense—had given a new impetus to my life—but he had not given me an ideal to which I could give my whole being. That Vivekananda gave me.

For days, weeks, months I pored over his works. His letters as well as his speeches from Colombo to Almora, replete as they were with practical advice to his countrymen, inspired me most. From this study I emerged with a vivid idea of the essence of his teachings. "Atmano Mokshartham Jagaddhitaya"—for your own salvation and for the service of humanity—that was to be life's goal. Neither the selfish monasticism of the middle ages, nor the modern utilitarianism of Bentham and Mill, could be a perfect ideal. And the service of Humanity included, of course, the service of one's country—for, as his biographer and his chief disciple, Sister Nivedita, pointed out,[2] "The queen of his adoration was his motherland . . There was not a cry within

[1] S. C. M.

[2] See her book, *The Master as I Saw Him.*

her shores that did not find in him a responsive echo." The Swami himself in one of his passionate utterances had said, "Say brothers at the top of your voice—the naked Indian, the illiterate Indian, the Brahman Indian, the Pariah Indian is my brother." Talking of the future, he had remarked that the Brahman (religious caste), the Kshatriya (warrior caste) and the Vaisya (trader caste) each had had their day and now came the turn of the Sudras, the down-trodden masses. To the ancient scriptures he had given a modern interpretation. Strength, strength, is what the Upanishads[1] say, he had often declared; have faith (shraddha) in yourselves as Nachiketa[2] of old had. To some idle monks he had turned round and said, "Salvation will come through football and not through the Gita."[3]

I was barely fifteen when Vivekananda entered my life. Then there followed a revolution within and everything was turned upside down. It was, of course, a long time before I could appreciate the full significance of his teachings or the greatness of his personality, but certain impressions were stamped indelibly on my mind from the outset. Both from his portraits as well as from his teachings, Vivekananda appeared before me as a full-blown personality. Many of the questions which vaguely stirred my mind, and of which I was to become conscious later on, found in him a satisfactory solution. My headmaster's personality ceased to be big enough to serve as my ideal. I had previously thought of studying philosophy as he had done and of emulating him. Now I thought of the path which Vivekananda had indicated.

[1] The Upanishads are the philosophical portion of the ancient scriptures, the Vedas.

[2] The son of one of the ancient sages of India.

[3] The Gita or Bhagavad Gita contains the essence of Hindu philosophy and may be regarded as the Bible of the Hindus.

From Vivekananda I turned gradually to his master, Ramakrishna Paramahansa. Vivekananda had made speeches, written letters, and published books which were available to the layman. But Ramakrishna, who was almost an illiterate man, had done nothing of the kind. He had lived his life and had left it to others to explain it. Nevertheless, there were books or diaries published by his disciples which gave the essence of his teachings as learnt from conversations with him. The most valuable element in these books was his practical direction regarding character-building in general and spiritual uplift in particular. He would repeat unceasingly that only through renunciation was realisation possible—that without complete self-abnegation spiritual development was impossible to acquire. There was nothing new in his teaching, which is as old as Indian civilisation itself, the Upanishads having taught thousands of years ago that through abandonment of worldly desires alone can immortal life be attained. The effectiveness of Ramakrishna's appeal lay, however, in the fact that he had practised what he preached and that, according to his disciples, he had reached the acme of spiritual progress.

The burden of Ramakrishna's precepts was—renounce lust and gold. This two-fold renunciation was for him the test of a man's fitness for spiritual life. The complete conquest of lust involved the sublimation of the sex-instinct, whereby to a man every woman would appear as mother.

I was soon able to get together a group of friends (besides my relative S.C.M.) who became interested in Ramakrishna and Vivekananda. At school and outside, whenever we had a chance, we would talk of nothing else but this topic. Gradually we took to long walks and excursions which would give us greater opportunities for meeting and discussion. Our numbers began to swell and we had a welcome acquisition in a young student[1] with a spiritual bent of mind who could sing devotional songs with deep fervour.

At home and abroad we began to attract attention. That was inevitable because of our eccentricities. Students did not, however, venture to ridicule us, because our prestige was high, as some of us occupied the top places at school. But such was not the case at home. My parents noticed before long that I was going out frequently in the company of other boys. I was questioned, warned in a friendly manner, and ultimately rebuked. But all to no purpose. I was rapidly changing and was no longer the goody-goody boy afraid of displeasing his parents. I had a new ideal before me now which had inflamed my soul—to effect my own salvation and to serve humanity by abandoning all worldly desires and breaking away from all undue restraints. I no longer recited Sanskrit verses inculcating obedience to one's parents; on the contrary, I took to verses which preached defiance.[2]

I doubt if I have passed through a more trying period in my life than now. Ramakrishna's example of renunciation and purity entailed a battle royal with all the forces of the lower self. And Vivekananda's ideal brought me into conflict with the existing family and social order. I was weak, the fight was a long-drawn one in which success was not easy to obtain, hence tension and unhappiness with occasional fits of depression.

[1] H. M. S.

[2] "You, Divine Mother, are my only refuge—neither father nor mother; neither friend nor brother, etc."

It is difficult to say which aspect of the conflict was more painful—the external or the internal. A stronger or less sensitive mind than mine would have come out successful more quickly or suffered much less acutely than I did. But there was no help, I had to go through what was in store for me. The more my parents endeavoured to restrain me, the more rebellious I became. When all other attempts failed, my mother took to tears. But even that had no effect on me. I was becoming callous, perhaps eccentric, and more determined to go my own way, though all the time I was feeling inwardly unhappy. To defy my parents in this way was contrary to my nature and to cause them pain was disagreeable, but I was swept onwards as by an irresistible current. There was very little appreciation or understanding at home of what I was dreaming at the time, and that added to my misery. The only solace was to be found in the company of friends and I began to feel more at home when away from home.

Studies began to lose their importance for me and, but for the fact that for years I had studied hard, I would have gone under. The only thing that now mattered to me was mental or spiritual exercise. I had no proper guide at the time and turned to books for such help as they could afford me. Only later did I realise that not all of these were written by reliable or experienced men. There were books on Brahmacharya or sex-control, which were readily made use of. Then there were books on meditation which were greedily devoured. Books on Yoga and especially Hatha-Yoga[1] were eagerly hunted

[1] Yoga means literally "Union" (with Godhead). The word "Yoga" is used, however, to indicate not merely the goal but also the means. Yogic practice has two branches—"Raja-Yoga" and "Hatha-Yoga". "Raja-Yoga" is concerned with the control of the mind and "Hatha-Yoga" with that of the body.

after and utilised. And, over and above this, all kinds of experiments were made. A faithful narration of all that I went through would suffice to make a first-class entertainment. Small wonder that some thought that I was on the verge of lunacy.

The first time I resolved to sit down in the Yogic fashion, the problem was how to do it without being seen and how to face ridicule should I be discovered during the act. The best thing was to attempt it in the dark after sunset, and so I did. But I was ultimately seen one day and there was a titter. One night while I was meditating in secret, the maid happened to come in to make the bed and bumped against me in the dark. Imagine her surprise when she found that she had knocked against a lump of flesh.

Concentration was practised in many ways. A black circle was made in the centre of a white background and the eyes were brought to stare fixedly at it till the mind became a perfect blank. Gazing at the blue sky was occasionally practised, and what beat everything was staring at the scorching mid-day sun with eyes wide open. Self-mortification of various kinds was also resorted to—for instance, eating simple vegetarian food, getting up in the early hours of the morning, hardening the body to heat and cold, etc.

Much of this had to be done with as little publicity as possible, whether at home or outside. One of Ramakrishna's favourite maxims was: practise contemplation in a forest or in a quiet corner, in your house or in your own mind, so that none may observe you. The only people who may know of it are fellow-devotees or fellow-Yogis. After we had practised for some time what we considered to be Yoga, we began to compare notes. Ramakrishna had often referred to the inner psychic experiences, including extraordinary powers, which would come one's way as he progressed along the spiritual path and had warned his disciples against feeling elated over them or indulging in self-advertisement or self-enjoyment of any sort. These psychic experiences and powers had to be transcended if one wanted to reach the higher regions of spiritual consciousness. Even after some months' effort I found that I could not lay claim to any such experience. I had a feeling of confidence, and more peace of mind and self-control than before, but that was about all. Perhaps this is due to the want of a Guru (preceptor), thought I, since people say that Yoga cannot be practised without a Guru. So began my search for a Guru.

In India those who have given up the world and consecrated their whole life to spiritual effort sometimes adopt the life of a traveller (Paribrajak) or undertake an all-India pilgrimage. It is therefore not difficult to find them in the vicinity of holy places like Hardwar, Benares, Puri (or Jagannath) or Rameswaram. Owing to its proximity to Puri, Cuttack also attracted a large number of them. These monks[1] are of two classes—those who belong to some organisation, 'Ashrama' or 'Muth', and those who are entirely free, have no organisation behind them, and hate to get entangled in any way. Our group—for by now we had a definite group—became interested in all the Sadhus who happened to

[1] Also called Sannyasis, Sadhus or fakirs, though fakirs are generally Mohammedans by religion. These must be distinguished from priests. Among the Hindus, priests are an integral part of society. They are Brahmans and are generally married. They perform religious and social ceremonies for the ordinary householder. Sadhus, on the other hand, renounce caste and all their family relationship when they take holy orders. They do not as a rule perform religious or social ceremonies for householders. Their sole function is to show to others the path of spiritual progress. They may be regarded as outside the pale of social conventions.

visit the town, and if any member got information about any such visitor, he would pass it on to the rest. Various were the types whom we visited, but I must say that those of the hermit type were more likable. They would not care to have any disciples and would spurn money in any form. If they wanted to instruct anybody in Yoga, they would prefer those who like themselves had no worldly attachment at all. The Sadhus who belonged to an organisation or were themselves married men did not appeal to me. They would generally search for disciples among men of wealth and position who, when recruited, would be an acquisition to their organisation.

Once there came an old Sannyasi, more than ninety years old, the head of a well-known Ashrama of all-India repute, one of whose disciples was a leading medical practitioner of the town. It soon became the rage to visit him and we too joined the crowd. After doing obeisance to him we took our seats. He was very kind to us—in fact, affectionate—and we were drawn towards him. Some hymns were recited by his disciples to which we respectfully listened. At the end we were given printed copies of his teachings and were advised to follow them. We inwardly resolved to do so—at least I did. The first item was—eat neither fish nor flesh nor eggs. Our family diet was non-vegetarian, and it was not possible to adhere to vegetarian food without coming in for criticism and perhaps opposition. Nevertheless, I obeyed the mandate despite all obstruction. The second item was daily recitation of certain hymns. That was easy. But the next item was formidable—the practice of submissiveness to one's parents. We had to begin the day by doing obeisance (pranam) to our parents. The difficulty about doing this was a two-fold one. Firstly, there was never any practice to do daily obeisance to our parents. Secondly, I had passed the stage when I believed that obedience to one's parents was in itself a virtue. I was rather in a mood to defy every obstacle to my goal, no matter from what source it came. However, with a supreme effort of the will, I mastered myself and marching straight to my father in the morning, I made obeisance as instructed by my preceptor.[1] I can still recall the scene—how my father was taken aback at this unexpected sight. He asked me what was the matter, but without uttering a word I marched back after doing my duty. Up till now I have not the faintest notion of what he or my mother (who also had to undergo the same experience) thought of me at the time. It was nothing less than a torture every morning to muster sufficient strength of mind to go up to my parents and do obeisance to them. Members of the family or even servants must have wondered what had made the rebellious boy suddenly so submissive. Little did they know perhaps that behind this phenomenon was the hand of a Sadhu.

After some weeks, perhaps months, I began to question myself as to what I had gained from the above practice and, not being satisfied with the reply, I gave it up. I went back to the teachings of Ramakrishna and Vivekananda. No realisation without renunciation —I told myself again.

It would be a mistake to conclude that my conception of a religious life was restricted to the practice of individualistic Yoga. Though for some time I went crazy over Yogic exercise, it slowly dawned on me that for spiritual development social service was necessary. The idea came probably from Vivekananda for, as I

[1] Another friend of mine, H.M.S., kept me company in this.

have indicated above, he had preached the ideal of the service of humanity which included the service of one's country. But he had further enjoined on everyone to serve the poor, for according to him God often comes to us in the form of the poor and to serve the poor is to worship God. I remember that I became very liberal with beggars, fakirs, and Sadhus, and whenever any of them appeared before our house, I helped them with whatever came within my reach. I derived a peculiar satisfaction from the act of giving.

Before I was sixteen I had my first experience of what may be glorified with the appelation of village reconstruction work. We went to a village in the outskirts of the town with the object of attempting some service. We entered the village primary school and did some teaching. By the teachers and the villagers in general we were warmly welcomed and we felt greatly encouraged. We then proceeded to another village but met with a sad experience there. When we entered the village, the villagers who had seen us from a distance collected in a body and as we advanced, they began to retreat. It was difficult to get at them or to talk to them as friends. We were shocked to find that we were regarded not only as strangers but as suspicious characters or enemies, and it did not take us long to understand that whenever well-dressed men had come into the village they must have done so as tax-collectors or in some similar capacity, and had behaved in such a manner as to create this gulf between the villagers and ourselves. A few years later, I was to have a similar experience in some other villages in Orissa.

It would be correct to say that, as long as I was at school, I did not mature politically, though in other matters I was inclined to be precocious. This was due partly to my innate proclivity which pointed in a different direction, partly to the fact that Orissa was a political backwater, and partly to lack of inspiration within the family circle. Occasionally I did hear about the affairs of the Congress from my elder brothers, but that did not make any impression on me. The first bomb thrown in 1908 created a stir everywhere and we too were momentarily interested. At the P. E. School where I then was, our headmistress condemned the throwing of bombs. The matter was soon forgotten however. About the same time processions used to be brought out in the town to condemn the partition of Bengal and to propagate the cause of Swadeshi (Home-industry). They occasioned a mild interest, but politics was tabooed in our house—so we could not take part in any political activity. Our interest sometimes found expression in peculiar ways such as cutting out pictures of revolutionaries from the papers and hanging them up in our study. One day we had a visitor, a relative of ours and a police officer, who saw these pictures and complained to my father, with the result that before we returned from school the pictures were all removed, much to our chagrin.

Up till December 1911 I was politically so undeveloped that I sat for an essay competition on the King's (George V) Coronation. Though I generally stood first in English composition, I did not get the prize on this occasion. During the Christmas Vacation I went to Calcutta with the rest of the family when King George V visited that city, and I returned in an enthusiastic frame of mind.

The first political impetus I received was in 1912 from a student[1] about the same age as myself. He came

[1] H. K. S.

to Cuttack and Puri on a tour and was introduced to us by Headmaster Beni Madhav Das. Before he came, he was connected with a certain group[1] in Calcutta which had as its ideal—spiritual uplift and national service along constructive lines. His visit to Cuttack came off at a time when my mind was beginning to turn towards social and national problems. In our group there was a friend who was more interested in national service than in Yoga. Another friend was always dreaming of the Bengali soldier, Suresh Biswas, who had migrated to South America (I think it was Brazil) and had made a name for himself there. And as a stepping stone to such a career, this friend was practising wrestling while some of us were busy with Yoga. At a psychologically opportune moment, the visitor talked to us passionately about our duty to our country and about his group in Calcutta, and I was greatly impressed. It was good to be linked up with an organisation in the metropolis and we heartily welcomed his visit. On his return to Calcutta he made a report about us and not long after we received a communication from the head of the group. Thus began a connection which was to last several years.

As I approached the end of my school career, my religious impulse began to grow in intensity. Studies were no longer of primary importance. The members of our group would meet as frequently as possible and go out on excursions. We could thereby keep away from home and enjoy one another's company longer. As a rule, the teachers failed to inspire us—with the exception of one or two who were followers of Ramakrishna and Vivekananda. My parents' Guru[2] visited Cuttack

[1] The head of this group was one S.C.B. who was studying medicine.

[2] This was their first Guru. After his death they received initiation from another Guru.

about this time and, while he was there, was able to rouse my religious interest still further. But his inspiration did not go very far because he was not a 'Sannyasi'. Among the teachers there was only one who was politically minded and, when we were about to leave school, he congratulated me on deciding to go to Calcutta where I would meet people who could inspire me politically.

I believe that impressions received in early life linger long and, for good or for ill, have a potent influence on the mind of the growing child. I remember that in infancy I often used to hear stories of ghosts, either from servants or from older members of the family. One particular tree was pointed out as being the favourite abode of ghosts. These stories when narrated at night had a most chilling effect. On a moonlit night after hearing such a story it was easy to conjure up a ghost on a tree out of the play of light and shade. One of our servants—a Mohammedan cook—must have done as much, for one night he declared that he was possessed by some spirit. A sorcerer had to be called and the spirit exorcised. Such experiences were reinforced from other quarters. For instance, we had a Mohammedan coachman who would tell us how skilled he was in the art of exorcising spirits and how often his services were requisitioned for that purpose. According to him, he had to slit his forearm near the wrist and offer the spirit some blood as a parting drink. One could question his veracity, but the fact remains that we did see sometimes fresh incisions on his wrist as well as marks of old ones. He was also a bit of a Hakim[1] and would prepare quack

[1] There are two indigenous systems of medicine in India which are still in vogue—Ayurveda and Unani. Those who practise the former are called Kavirajes or Vaids, while those who practise the latter are called Hakims.

Continued on next page

remedies for various ailments like indigestion, diarrhoea, etc. I must say that such experience in infancy did not have a particular wholesome effect on my mind and it required an effort to overthrow such influences when I grew into boyhood.

In this task of freeing my mind of superstitions, Vivekananda was of great help to me. The religion that he preached—including his conception of Yoga—was based on a rational philosophy, on the Vedanta[1], and his conception of Vedanta was not antagonistic to, but was based on, scientific principles.[2] One of his missions in life was to bring about a reconciliation between science and religion, and this, he held, was possible through the Vedanta.

Those who tackle the problem of child education in India will have to consider the uncongenial influences which mould the child's mind at the present day. Of allied interest is the question of the lullaby songs which are sung by the mother, the aunt, or the nurse to rock the child to sleep or of the means adopted to induce an unwilling child to take its food. Too often the child is frightened into doing both. In Bengal one of the most popular lullaby songs describes the 'Bargis' (or the Pindari hordes) raiding the countryside

Continued from previous page
The Ayurvedic system comes down from the very ancient times, while the Unani system came into vogue at the time of the Moghul Emperors. Though there are many quacks practising these systems, there is no doubt that Kavirajes and Hakims sometimes effect wonderful cures where Western doctors fail.

[1] Vedanta is a general term for the philosophical portion of the Hindu Scriptures.

[2] It should be remembered that Vivekananda was trained in Western logic and philosophy and was inclined to be a sceptic and agnostic before he came under the influence of Ramakrishna. Since he had an emancipated mind, he could extract the essence of religion out of a mass of superstitions and mystical accretions in which it is sometimes found embedded in India.

after nightfall. Certainly not a congenial song for a sleepy child.

One will also have to consider the dreams which sometimes disturb the child's sleep and leave an effect on its waking life as well. A knowledge of the psychology and mechanism of dreams will enable the guardian or the tutor to understand the child's mind and thereby help it to overcome unwholesome influences preying on its mind. I say this because I myself was troubled greatly by frightful dreams about snakes, tigers, monkeys, and the like in my early years. Only when I began experimenting with Yoga in an empirical fashion later on, did I hit upon a mental exercise which relieved me of such unpleasant dreams[1] once for all.

It is possible in a country like India and especially in families where conservative, parochial, sectarian, or caste influences reign supreme, to grow into maturity and even obtain high University degrees without being really emancipated. It often happens, therefore, that at some stage or other one has to revolt against social or family conventions. I was lucky, however, that the environment in which I grew up was on the whole conducive to the broadening of my mind. In my infancy I was brought into touch with English people, English education, and English culture. After that I went back to our culture—both classical and modern—and even while I was at school had inter-provincial contacts and friendship which I would have been deprived of, if I had been living in Bengal. Lastly, my mental attitude towards Muslims in general was largely, though unconsciously, influenced by my early contacts. The quarter

[1] I shall have occasion to refer later on to other dreams which disturbed me from time to time, e.g., sex-dreams, dreams of university examination, dreams of arrest and imprisonment, etc.

in which we lived was a predominantly Muslim one and our neighbours were mostly Muslims. They all looked up to father as ordinary villagers do to a patriarch. We took part in their festivals, like the Moharrum, for instance, and enjoyed their akhara.[1] Among our servants were Muslims who were as devoted to us as the others. At school I had Muslim teachers and Muslim class-mates with whom my relations—as also the relations of other students—were perfectly cordial. In fact, I cannot remember ever to have looked upon Muslims as different from ourselves in any way, except that they go to pray in a mosque. And friction or conflict between Hindus and Muslims was unknown in my early days.

Though the atmosphere in which I grew up was on the whole liberalizing, there were occasions when I was forced into a clash with social or family conventions. I remember one incident when I was about fourteen or fifteen. A class friend[2] of mine who was also a neighbour of ours invited some of us to dinner. My mother came to know of it and gave instructions that no one was to go. It might have been because his social status was lower than ours, or because he belonged to a lower caste, or simply because on medical grounds it was considered inadvisable to dine out. And it is true that very rarely did we go anywhere for dinner. However, I regarded my mother's orders as unjustified and felt a peculiar pleasure in defying them. When I took to religion and Yoga seriously and wanted freedom to go where I liked and meet whomsoever I wished, I frequently came up against parental instructions. But I had no

[1] Physical sports which Muslims indulge in on the occasion of the Moharrum festival.

[2] D. N. D.

hesitation in disobeying them because by that time I believed, under the inspiration of Vivekananda, that revolt is necessary for self-fulfilment—that when a child is born, its very cry is a revolt against the bondage in which it finds itself.

Looking back on my school days I have no doubt that I must have appeared to others as wayward, eccentric, and obstinate. I was expected to do well at the Matriculation Examination and raise the prestige of the school and great must have been the disappointment of my teachers when they found me neglecting my studies and running after ash-laden Sadhus. What my parents must have thought and felt over a promising boy going off his head can best be imagined. But nothing mattered to me except my inner dreams, and the more resistance I met, the more obstinate I became. My parents then thought that a change of environment would perhaps do me good and that in the realistic atmosphere of Calcutta I would shed my eccentricities and take to a normal life like the rest of my tribe.

I sat for the Matriculation Examination in March, 1913 and came out second in the whole University. My parents were delighted and I was packed off to Calcutta.

CHAPTER SIX

PRESIDENCY COLLEGE (1)

Little did my people know what Calcutta had in store for me. I was separated from a small group of eccentric school-boys whom I had gathered round myself in Cuttack. But in Calcutta I found crowds of them. No wonder that I soon became the despair of my parents.

This was not my first visit to Calcutta. I had been there several times since my infancy, but every time this great city had intrigued me, bewildered me, beyond measure. I had loved to roam about its wide streets and among its gardens and museums and I had felt that one could not see enough of it. It was like a leviathan which one could look at from outside and go on admiring unceasingly. But this time I came to settle down there and to mix with its inner life. I did not, of course, know then that this was the beginning of a connection which would perhaps last all my life.

Life in Calcutta, like life in any other modern metropolis, is not good for everybody and it has been the ruin of many promising souls. It might have proved disastrous in my case, had not I come there with certain definite ideas and principles fixed in my mind. Though I was passing through a period of stormy transition when I left school, I had by then made certain definite decisions for myself—I was not going to follow the beaten track, come what may; I was going to lead a life conducive to my spiritual welfare and the uplift of humanity; I was going to make a profound study of philosophy so that I could solve the fundamental problems of life; in practical life I was going to emulate Ramakrishna and Vivekananda as far as possible and, in any case, I was not going in for a worldly career. This was the outlook with which I faced a new chapter in my life.

These decisions were not the offspring of one night's thought or the dictation of any one personality. It had taken me months and years of groping to arrive at them. I had looked into so many books and sat at the feet of so many persons in order to discover how my life should be shaped and what the highest ideals were that I could hold up before myself. The discovery would have been easy and the task of translating it into action still easier if I had not been pulled by my lower self in one direction and by family influence in another. Owing to this double tension the latter portion of my school life was a period of intense mental conflict and of consequent unhappiness. The conflict itself was nothing new. Everybody who sets up an ideal before himself or endeavours to strike out a new path has to go through it. But my suffering was unusually acute for two reasons. Firstly, the struggle overtook me too early in life. Secondly, the two conflicts came upon me simultaneously. If I had encountered them consecutively, the agony would have been greatly alleviated. But man is not always the architect of his fate, he is sometimes the creature of his circumstances.

The strain of a fight on two fronts was so great for a highly-strung lad like myself that it was quite on the cards that I would have ended in a breakdown or in some mental aberration. That I did not do so was due either to sheer luck or to some higher destiny, if one believes in it. Now that I have come out of the ordeal comparatively unscathed, I do not regret what I have been through. I have this consolation to offer myself that the struggle made a man of me. I gained self-confidence, which I had lacked before and I succeeded in determining some of the fundamental principles of my life. From my experience, I may, however, warn parents and guardians that they should be circumspect in dealing with children possessing an emotional and sensitive nature. It is no use trying to force them into a particular groove, for the more they are suppressed, the more rebellious they become and this rebelliousness may ultimately develop into rank waywardness. On the other hand, sympathetic understanding combined with a certain amount of latitude may cure them of angularities and idiosyncrasies. And when they are drawn towards an idea which militates against worldly notions, parents and guardians should not attempt to thwart or ridicule them, but endeavour to understand them and through understanding to influence them should the need arise.

Whatever may be the ultimate truth about such notions as God, soul and religion, from the purely pragmatic point of view I may say that I was greatly benefited by my early interest in religion and my dabbling in Yoga. I learnt to take life seriously. Standing on the threshold of my college career, I felt convinced that life had a meaning and a purpose. To fulfil that purpose, a regular schooling of the body and the mind was necessary. But for this self-imposed schooling during my school-life, I doubt if I would have succeeded in facing the trials and tribulations of my later years, in view of the delicate constitution with which I had been endowed from my birth.

I have indicated before that up to a certain stage in my life I had fitted into my environment splendidly and accepted all the social and moral values imposed from without. This happens in the life of every human being. Then there comes a stage of doubt—not merely intellectual doubt like that of Descartes—but doubt embracing the whole of life. Man begins to question his very existence—why he was born, for what purpose he lives, and what his ultimate goal is. If he comes to a definite conclusion, whether of a permanent or of a temporary nature, on such problems, it often happens that his outlook on life changes—he begins to view everything from a different perspective and goes in for a revaluation of existing social and moral values. He builds up a new world of thought and morality within himself and, armed with it, he faces the external world. Thereafter, he either succeeds in moulding his environment in the direction of his ideal or fails in the struggle and succumbs to reality as he finds it.

It depends entirely on a man's psychic constitution how far his doubt will extend and to what extent he would like to reconstruct his inner life, as a stepping stone towards the reconstruction of reality. In this respect, each individual is a law unto himself (or herself). But in one matter we stand on common ground. No great achievement, whether internal or external, is possible without a revolution in one's life. And this revolution has two stages—the stage of doubt or scepticism and the stage of reconstruction. It is not absolutely necessary for revolutionising our practical life—whether individual or collective—that we should tackle the more fundamental problems, in relation to which we may very well have an agnostic attitude. From the very ancient times, both in the East and in the West, there have been schools of philosophy and ethics based on materialism or agnosticism. In my own case, however, the religious pursuit was a pragmatic necessity. The intellectual doubt which assailed me needed satisfaction and, constituted as I then was, that satisfaction would not have been possible without some rational philosophy. The philosophy which I found in Vivekananda and in Ramakrishna came nearest to meeting my requirements and offered a basis on which to reconstruct my moral and practical life. It equipped me with certain principles with which to determine my conduct or line of action whenever any problem or crisis arose before my eyes.

That does not mean that all my doubts were set at rest once for all. Unfortunately, I am not so unsophisticated as that. Moreover, progress in life means a series of doubts followed by a series of attempts at resolving them.

Perhaps the most bitter struggle I had with myself was in the domain of sex-instinct. It required practically no effort on my part to decide that I should not adopt a career of self-preferment, but should devote my life to some noble cause. It required some effort to school myself, physically and mentally, for a life of service and unavoidable hardship. But it required an unceasing effort, which continues till today, to suppress or sublimate the sex-instinct.

Avoidance of sexual indulgence and even control of active sex-desire is, I believe, comparatively easy to attain. But for one's spiritual development, as understood by Indian Yogis and Saints, that is not enough. The mental background—the life of instinct and impulse—out of which sex-desire arises has to be transformed. When this is achieved, a man or woman loses all sex-appeal and becomes impervious to the sex-appeal of others; he transcends sex altogether. But is it possible or is it only midsummer madness? According to Ramakrishna it is possible, and until one attains this level of chastity, the highest reaches of spiritual consciousness remain inaccessible to him. Ramakrishna, we are told, was often put to the test by people who doubted his spirituality and mental purity, but on every occasion that he was thrown in the midst of attractive women, his reactions were non-sexual. In the company of women, he could feel as an innocent child feels in the presence of its mother. Ramakrishna used always to say that gold and sex are the two greatest obstacles in the path of spiritual development and I took his words as gospel truth.

In actual practice the difficulty was that the more I concentrated on the suppression or sublimation of the sex-instinct, the stronger it seemed to become, at least in the initial stages. Certain psycho-physical exercises, including certain forms of meditation, were helpful in acquiring sex-control. Though I gradually made progress, the degree of purity which Ramakrishna had insisted on, seemed impossible to reach. I persisted in spite of temporary fits of depression and remorse, little knowing at the time how natural the sex-instinct was to the human mind. As I desired to continue the struggle for the attainment of perfect purity, it followed that I had to visualise the future in terms of a celibate life.

It is now a moot question whether we should spend so much of our time and energy in trying to eradicate or sublimate an instinct which is as inherent in human nature as in animal life. Purity and continence in boyhood and in youth are of course necessary, but what Ramakrishna and Vivekananda demanded was much more than that, nothing less than complete transcending of sex-consciousness. Our stock of physical and psychic energy is, after all, limited. Is it worth while expending so much of it in an endeavour to conquer sex? Firstly, is complete conquest of sex, that is, a complete transcending or sublimation of the sex-instinct, indispensable to spiritual advancement? Secondly, even if it is, what is the relative importance of sex-control[1] in a life which is devoted not so much to spiritual development as to social service—the greatest good of the greatest number? Whatever the answer to these two questions may be, in the year 1918 when I joined College, it was almost a fixed idea with me that conquest of sex was essential to spiritual progress, and that without spiritual uplift human life had little or no value. But though I was at grips with the demon of sex-instinct, I was still far from getting it under control.

If I could live my life over again, I should not in all probability give sex the exaggerated importance which I did in my boyhood and youth. That does not mean that I regret what I did. If I did err in overemphasising the importance of sex-control, I probably erred on the right side, for certain benefits did accrue therefrom —though perhaps incidentally. For instance, it made me prepare myself for a life which did not follow the beaten track and in which there was no room for ease, comfort, and self-aggrandisement.

To resume my story, I joined the Presidency College, then regarded as the premier College of the Calcutta University. I had three months' holiday before the colleges were to reopen after the summer vacation. But I lost no time in getting into touch with

[1] As I have gradually turned from a purely spiritual ideal to a life of social service, my views on sex have undergone transformation.

that group, an emissary of which I had met a year ago in Cuttack. A lad of sixteen usually feels lost in a big city like Calcutta, but such was not the case with me. Before the College opened I had made myself at home in Calcutta and found a number of friends of my choice.

The first few days of College life were interesting to a degree. The standard of the Matriculation Examination being lower in Indian than in British Universities, Indian matriculates enter College earlier than British boys do. I was barely sixteen and a half years old when I walked into the precincts of Presidency College; nevertheless, like so many others, I felt as if I was suddenly entering into man's estate. That was indeed a pleasurable feeling. We had ceased to be boys and were now men. The first few days were spent in taking stock of our class-mates and sizing them up. Everybody seemed to be anxious to have a look at those who had come out at the top. Hailing from a district town I was inclined to be shy and reserved at first. Some of the students coming from Calcutta schools, like the Hindu and Hare Schools, had a tendency to be snobbish and give themselves airs. But they could not carry on like that, because the majority of the higher places at the Matriculation Examination had been captured by boys from other schools and, moreover, we were soon able to hold our own against the metropolitans.

Before long I began to look out for men of my own way of thinking among my class-mates. Birds of a feather flock together—so I managed to get such a group. It was unavoidable that we should attract a certain amount of attention because we consciously wore a puritanic exterior; but we did not care. In those days one could observe several groups[1] among the College students, each with a distinctive character. There was firstly a group consisting of the sons of Rajas and rich folks and those who preferred to hobnob with them. They dressed well and took a dilettante interest in studies. Then there was a group of bookworms—well-meaning, goody-goody boys with sallow faces and thick glasses. Thirdly, there was a group similar to ours consisting of earnest boys who considered themselves the spiritual heirs of Ramakrishna and Vivekananda. Last but not least, there existed a secret group of revolutionaries about whose existence most of the students were quite unaware. The character of Presidency College itself was different from what it is now.[2] Though it was a Government institution, the students as a rule were anything but loyalist. This was due to the fact that the best students were admitted into the College without any additional recommendation and regardless of their parentage. In the councils of the C.I.D.,[3] the Presidency College students had a bad name—so ran the rumour. The main hostel of the College, known as the Eden Hindu Hostel, was looked upon as a hot-bed of sedition, a rendezvous of revolutionaries, and was frequently searched by the police.

For the first two years of my College life I was greatly under the influence of the group referred to above and I developed intellectually during this period. The group consisted mainly of students, the leaders being two students of the Medical College.[4] It followed generally the teachings of Ramakrishna and

[1] Sometimes these groups ran into one another.

[2] The presence of men like the late Sir J. C. Bose and Sir P. C. Ray among the professorial staff also had some effect.

[3] India's Scotland Yard (Criminal Investigation Department).

[4] S.C.B. and K.K.A.

Vivekananda but emphasised social service as a means to spiritual development. It interpreted social service not in terms of building hospitals and charitable dispensaries, as the followers of Vivekananda were inclined to do, but as national reconstruction, mainly in the educational sphere.[1] Vivekananda's teachings had been neglected by his own followers—by the Ramakrishna Mission which he had founded—and we were going to give effect to them. We could therefore be called the neo-Vivekananda group, and our main object was to bring about a synthesis between religion and nationalism, not merely in the theoretical sphere but in practical life as well. The emphasis on nationalism was inevitable in the political atmosphere of Calcutta of those days.

When I left Cuttack in 1918 my ideas were altogether nebulous. I had a spiritual urge and a vague idea of social service of some sort. In Calcutta I learnt that social service was an integral part of Yoga and it meant not merely relief to the half, the maimed, and the blind, but national reconstruction on modern lines. Beyond this stage, the group did not travel for a long time, because like myself it was groping for more light and for a clarification of its practical ideals. There was one thing highly creditable about the group—its members were exceedingly alert and active, many of them being brilliant scholars. The activity of the group manifested itself in three directions. There was a thirst for new ideas; so new books on philosophy, history, and nationalism were greedily devoured and the information thus acquired was passed on to others. Members of the group were also active in recruiting new members from different institutions in various cities, with the result that before long the group had wide contacts. Thirdly,

[1] Possibly the example of the Christian Missionaries had some influence.

the members were active in making contacts with the prominent personalities of the day. Holidays would be utilised for visiting the holy cities like Benares or Hardwar with the hope of meeting men who could give spiritual light and inspiration, while those interested in national history would visit places of historical importance and study history on the spot. I once joined a touring party who journeyed for seven days, book in hand, in the environs of Murshidabad, the pre-British capital of Bengal, and we thereby acquired more insight into the previous history of Bengal than we would have done if we had studied at home or at school for months.

On some important questions the ideas of the group were in a state of flux. Such was the question of our relations with our respective families. The name, constitution, plan of work, etc. of the group were not settled either. But our ideas slowly moved in the direction of a first-class educational institution which would turn out real men and would have branches in different places. Some members of the group interested themselves in the study of existing educational institutions like Tagore's Santi-Niketan and the Gurukul University in Upper India. In recruiting new members, attention was given to enlisting brilliant students studying different subjects, so that we would have trained professors in all the subjects when the time came for us to launch our scheme. The group stood for celibacy and the leaders held that a breach with one's family was inevitable at some stage or other. But the members were not given any clear direction to break with their families, though the way they moved about made it inevitable that their families would be estranged. Most of the week-ends were spent away from home, often without permission. Sometimes institutions like the

Ramakrishna Mission's Muth at Belur would be visited. Sometimes important personalities,[1] generally religious people, would be interviewed. Sometimes our own members in different places would invite us and we would spend a day or two with them. Outside college hours most of my time would be spent in the company of members of the group. Home had no attraction for me—for it was a world quite different from that of my dreams. The dualism in my life continued and it was a source of unhappiness. This was accentuated whenever unfavourable comments were made at home about my ideas or activities.

Politically, the group was against terroristic activity and secret conspiracy of every sort. The group was therefore not so popular among the students, for in those days the terrorist-revolutionary movement had a peculiar fascination for the students of Bengal. Even those who would keep at a safe distance from such an organisation would not withold their sympathy and admiration, so long as they did not land themselves in trouble. Occasionally there would be friction between members of our group and members of some terrorist-revolutionary organisations engaged in recruiting. Once a very interesting incident took place. Since our group was very active, the C.I.D. became very suspicious about its real character, wondering if there was anything hidden behind a religious exterior. Steps were taken to arrest a member whom they considered to be the leader of the group. At this juncture the police intercepted some correspondence passing between members of a terrorist-revolutionary organisation, in which there

[1] We visited the poet Rabindra Nath Tagore also and he gave a discourse on village reconstruction. This was in 1914, years before the Congress took up this work.

was a proposal to liquidate the above leader of our group for luring away some of its members into the path of non-violence. The correspondence revealed our real character to the police and thereby not only prevented the arrest but saved us from police persecution which would otherwise have been unavoidable. In the winter of 1918 we had a camp at Santipur, a place 50 miles from Calcutta on the river Hooghly, where we lived as monks wearing orange-coloured cloths. We were raided by the police and all our names and addresses were taken down, but no serious trouble followed beyond an enquiry into our antecedents.

In my undergraduate days Arabindo Ghose was easily the most popular leader in Bengal, despite his voluntary exile and absence since 1909. His was a name to conjure with. He had sacrificed a lucrative career in order to devote himself to politics. On the Congress platform he had stood up as a champion of left-wing thought and a fearless advocate of independence at a time when most of the leaders, with their tongues in their cheeks, would talk only of colonial self-government. He had undergone incarceration with perfect equanimity. His close association with Lokamanya B. G. Tilak[1] had given him an all-India popularity, while rumour and official allegation had given him an added prestige in the eyes of the younger generation by connecting him with his younger brother, Barindra Kumar Ghose, admittedly the pioneer of the terrorist movement. Last but not least, a mixture of spirituality and politics had given him a halo of mysticism and made his personality more fascinating to those who were

[1] Lokamanya Tilak was popularly known as 'Bardada' or Elder Brother and Arabindo as 'Chotdada' or Younger Brother. Tilak was the leader of the left-wing or 'extremist' party in the Congress.

religiously inclined. When I came to Calcutta in 1918, Arabindo was already a legendary figure. Rarely have I seen people speak of a leader with such rapturous enthusiasm and many were the anecdotes of this great man, some of them probably true, which travelled from mouth to mouth. I heard, for instance, that Arabindo had been in the habit of indulging in something like automatic writing. In a state of semi-trance, pencil in hand, he would have a written dialogue with his own self, giving him the name of 'Manik'. During his trial, the police came across some of the papers in which the 'conversations' with 'Manik' were recorded, and one day the police prosecutor, who was excited over the discovery, stood up before the Court and gravely asked for a warrant against a new conspirator, 'Manik', to the hilarious amusement of the gentlemen in the dock.

In those days it was freely rumoured that Arabindo had retired to Pondicherry for twelve years' meditation. At the end of that period he would return to active life as an 'enlightened' man, like Gautama Buddha of old, to effect the political salvation of his country. Many people seriously believed this, especially those who felt that it was well nigh impossible to successfully contend with the British people on the physical plane without the aid of some supernatural force. It is highly interesting to observe how the human mind resorts to spiritual nostrums when it is confronted with physical difficulties of an insurmountable character. When the big agitation started after the partition of Bengal in 1905, several mystic stories were in circulation. It was said, for instance, that on the final day of reckoning with the British there would be a 'march of the blanketeers' into Fort William in Calcutta. Sannyasis or fakirs with blankets on their shoulders would enter the Fort. The

British troops would stand stock-still, unable to move or fight, and power would pass into the hands of people. Wish is father to the thought and we loved to hear and to believe such stories in our boyhood.

As a College student it was not the mysticism surrounding Arabindo's name which attracted me, but his writings and also his letters. Arabindo was then editing a monthly journal called *Arya* in which he expounded his philosophy. He used also to write to certain select people in Bengal. Such letters would pass rapidly from hand to hand, especially in circles interested in spirituality-cum-politics. In our circle usually somebody would read the letter aloud and the rest of us would enthuse over it. In one such letter Arabindo wrote, 'We must be dynamos of the divine electricity so that when each of us stands up, thousands around may be full of the light—full of bliss and Ananda.' We felt convinced that spiritual enlightenment was necessary for effective national service.

But what made a lasting appeal to me was not such flashy utterances. I was impressed by his deeper philosophy. Shankara's doctrine of Maya was like a thorn in my flesh. I could not accommodate my life to it nor could I easily get rid of it. I required another philosophy to take its place. The reconciliation between the One and the Many, between God and Creation, which Ramakrishna and Vivekananda had preached, had indeed impressed me but had not till then succeeded in liberating me from the cobwebs of Maya. In this task of emancipation, Arabindo came as an additional help. He worked out a reconciliation between Spirit and Matter, between God and Creation, on the metaphysical side and supplemented it with a synthesis of the methods of attaining the truth—a synthesis of Yoga, as he called it.

Thousands of years ago the Bhagavad Gita had spoken about the different Yogas—Jnana Yoga or the attainment of truth through knowledge; Bhakti Yoga or the attainment of truth through devotion and love; Karma Yoga or the attainment of truth through selfless action. To this, other schools of Yoga had been added later—Hatha Yoga aiming at control over the body and Raja Yoga aiming at control over the mind through control of the breathing apparatus. Vivekananda had no doubt spoken of the need of Jnana (knowledge), Bhakti (devotion and love) and Karma (selfless action) in developing an all-round character, but there was something original and unique in Arabindo's conception of a synthesis of Yoga. He tried to show how by a proper use of the different Yogas one could rise step by step to the highest truth. It was so refreshing, so inspiring, to read Arabindo's writings as a contrast to the denunciation of knowledge and action by the later-day Bengal Vaishnavas. All that was needed in my eyes to make Arabindo an ideal guru for mankind was his return to active life.

Of quite a different type from Arabindo was Surendra Nath Bennerji, once the hero of Bengal and certainly one of the makers of the Indian National Congress. I saw him for the first time at a meeting of the Calcutta Town Hall[1] in connection with Mahatma Gandhi's Satyagraha[2] campaign in South Africa. Surendra Nath was still in good form and with his modulated voice and rolling periods he was able to collect a large sum of money at the meeting. But despite his flowery rhetoric and consummate oratory, he lacked that deeper passion which one could find in such simple words of

[1] This was probably towards the end of 1913 or the beginning of 1914.
[2] This may be paraphrased as 'passive resistance' or 'civil disobedience'.

Arabindo: 'I should like to see some of you becoming great; great not for your own sake, but to make India great, so that she may stand up with head erect amongst the free nations of the world. Those of you who are poor and obscure—I should like to see their poverty and obscurity devoted to the service of the motherland. Work that she might prosper, suffer that she might rejoice'.[1]

So long as politics did not interest me, my attention was directed towards two things—meeting as many religious teachers as possible and qualifying for social service. I doubt if there was any religious group or sect in or near Calcutta with whom we did not come into contact. With regard to social service, I had some novel and interesting experience. When I became eager to do some practical work, I found out a society for giving aid to the poor. This society[2] used to collect money and foodstuffs every Sunday by begging from door to door. The begging used to be done by student-volunteers and I became one of them. The collections used to consist mainly of rice, and each volunteer had to bring in between 80 and 160 lbs. of rice at the end of his round. The first day I went out sack in hand for collecting rice, I had to overcome forcibly a strong sense of shame, not having been accustomed to this sort of work. Up to this day I do not know if the members of our family were ever aware of this activity of mine. The sense of shame troubled me for a long time and, whenever there was any fear of coming across a known face, I simply did not look to the right or to the left but jogged along with the sack in my hand or over my shoulders.

[1] An extract from a political speech of Arabindo which my eldest brother was fond of repeating.

[2] The Anath Bhandar of South Calcutta.

At College I began to neglect my studies. Most of the lectures were uninteresting[1] and the professors still more so. I would sit absent-minded and go on philosophizing about the why and wherefore of such futile studies. Most boring of all was the professor of mathematics whose monotonous drawling out of what appeared to be meaningless formulae would bring me to the verge of desperation. To make life more interesting and purposeful, I engaged in various public activities of the student community, barring sports of course. I also went out of my way to get acquainted with such professors as Sir P. C. Ray, the eminent chemist and philanthropist, who did not belong to our department but was extremely popular with the students. Organising debates, collecting funds for flood and famine relief, representing the students before the authorities, going out on excursions with fellow-students—such activities were most congenial to me. Very slowly I was shedding my introvert tendencies and social service was gaining ground on the individualistic Yoga.

I sometimes wonder how at a particular psychological moment a small incident can exert a far-reaching influence on our life. In front of our house in Calcutta, an old, decrepit beggar woman used to sit every day and beg for alms. Every time I went out or came in, I could not help seeing her. Her sorrowful countenance and her tattered clothes pained me whenever I looked at her or even thought of her. By contrast, I appeared to be so well-off and comfortable that I used to feel like a criminal. What right had I—I used to think—to be so fortunate to live in a three-storied house when this miserable beggar woman had hardly a roof over her head

[1] This impression must have been due partly to the fact that my interest in studies had flagged.

and practically no food or clothing? What was the value of Yoga if so much misery was to continue in the world? Thoughts like these made me rebel against the existing social system.

But what could I do? A social system could not be demolished or transformed in a day. Something had to be done for this beggar woman in the meantime and that unobtrusively. I used to get money from home for going to and returning from College by tramcar. This I resolved to save and spend in charity. I would often walk back from College—a distance of over three miles—and sometimes even walk to it when there was sufficient time. This lightened my guilty conscience to some extent.

During my first year in College I returned to Cuttack to spend the vacations there with my parents. My Calcutta record was much worse than my Cuttack record, so there was no harm in letting me return to my friends there. At Cuttack, though I had regularly roamed about with my friends, I had never absented myself from home at night. But in Calcutta I would often be absent for days without obtaining permission. On returning to Cuttack, I got into my old set again. Once, when my parents were out of town, I was invited to join a party of friends who were going into the interior on a nursing expedition in a locality which was stricken with cholera. There was no medical man in the party. We had only a half-doctor, whose belongings consisted of a book on homoeopathy, a box of homoeopathic medicines, and plenty of common sense. We were to be the nurses in the party. I readily agreed and took leave of my uncle, who was then doing duty for my father, saying that I would be away a few days. He did not object, not knowing at the time that I was going out to nurse cholera patients. I was out for only a week, as my uncle came to know of our real plans a few days after I had left and sent another uncle post-haste after me to bring me back. The searching party had to scour the countryside before they could spot us.

In those days cholera was regarded as a fatal disease and it was not easy to get people to attend cholera patients. Our party was absolutely fearless in that respect. In fact, we took hardly any precautions against infection and we all lived and dined together. In the way of actual medical relief, I do not think we could give much. Many had died before we arrived there and, among the patients we found and nursed, the majority did not recover. Nevertheless, a week's experience opened a new world before my eyes and unfolded a picture of real India, the India of the villages—where poverty stalks over the land, men die like flies, and illiteracy is the prevailing order. We had very little with us in the way of bedding and clothing, because we had to travel light in order to be able to cover long distances on foot. We ate what we could get in the way of food and slept where we could. For me, one of the most astonishing things was the surprise with which we were greeted when we first arrived on the scene of our humanitarian efforts. It intrigued the poor villagers to know why we had come there. Were we Government officials? Officials had never come to nurse them before. Neither had well-to-do people from the town bothered about them. They therefore concluded that we must have undertaken this tour in order to acquire reputation or merit. It was virtually impossible to knock this idea out of their heads.

When I was back in Calcutta the craze for 'Sadhu'-hunting continued. About sixty miles from the city, on the bank of a river near a district town, there lived a young ascetic hailing from the Punjab. Along with a friend of mine[1] I would visit him frequently whenever I could get away from Calcutta. This ascetic would never take shelter under a roof, for the ideal which he evidently practised was

> "The sky the roof, the grass the bed
> And food what chance may bring."

I was greatly impressed by this man—his complete renunciation of worldly desires, his utter indifference to heat, cold,[2] etc., his mental purity and loving temperament. He would never ask for anything, but as often happens in India, crowds[3] would come to him and offer food and clothing, and he would take only his minimum requirements. If only he had been more intellectually developed, he could have lured me from my worldly moorings.

After I came into contact with this ascetic, the desire to find a guru grew stronger and stronger within me and, in the summer vacation of 1914, I quietly left on a pilgrimage with another friend[4] of mine. I borrowed some money from a class friend who was getting a scholarship and repaid him later from my scholarship. Of course, I did not inform anybody at home and simply wrote a postcard when I was far away. We visited some of the well-known places of pilgrimage in Upper India—Lachman-Jhola, Hrishikesh, Hardwar,

[1] H. K. S.

[2] When it was about midday, he would light five fires (Panchagni) and sitting in the middle would practise meditation in the scorching sun. He told me that snakes would often crawl over his body at night but that did not disturb his sleep.

[3] Among his visitors were the C.I.D. who wanted to know if he was merely a harmless ascetic.

[4] H. P. C.

Muttra, Brindaban, Benares, Gaya. At Hardwar we were joined by another friend. In between we also visited places of historical interest like Delhi and Agra. At all these places we looked up as many Sadhus as we could and visited several 'Ashramas'[1] as well as educational institutions like Gurukul and Rishikul.[2] At one of the Ashramas in Hardwar they felt uncomfortable when we went there, not knowing if we were really spiritually minded youths or were Bengalee revolutionaries appearing in that cloak. This tour which lasted nearly two months brought us in touch not only with a number of holy men, but also with some of the patent shortcomings of Hindu society, and I returned home a wiser man, having lost much of my admiration for ascetics and anchorites. It was well that I had this experience off my own bat, for in life there are certain things which we have to learn for ourselves.

The first shock that I received was when, at an eating-house in Hardwar, they refused to serve us food. Bengalees, they said, were unclean like Christians because they ate fish. We could bring our plates and they would pour out the food, but we would have to go back to our lodging and eat there. Though one of my friends was a Brahman, he too had to eat humble pie. At Buddha-Gaya we had a similar experience. We were guests at a Muth to which we have been introduced by the head of the Ramakrishna Mission at Benares. When we were to take our food we were asked if we would not like to sit separately, because all of us were not of the same caste. I expressed my surprise at this question because

[1] These are homes for ascetics. Nowadays there are also Ashramas for political workers.

[2] These are institutions based on ancient Hindu ideals. The Gurukul being connected with the Arya Samaj is naturally more reformist in outlook than the Rishikul, especially in the matter of caste.

they were followers of Shankaracharya, and I quoted a verse[1] of his in which he had advised people to give up all sense of difference. They could not challenge my statement because I was on strong ground. The next day when we went for a bath we were told by some men there not to draw the water from the well because we were not Brahmans. Fortunately, my Brahman friend, who was in the habit of hanging his sacred thread on a peg, had it on him at the moment. With a flourish he pulled it out from under his *chaddar* and just to defy them he began to draw the water and pass it on to us, much to their discomfiture.[2]

At Muttra we lived in the house of a Panda[3] and visited a hermit who was living in an underground room on the other bank of the river. He strongly advised us to return home and to give up all ideas of renouncing the world. I remember I was greatly annoyed at a hermit speaking in that fashion. While we were at Muttra we became very friendly with an Arya Samajist[4] living next door. This was too much for our Panda who gave us a warning that these Arya Samajists were dangerous men since they denounced image-worship.

The monkeys at Muttra who could not be kept down in any way, were a regular pest. If any door or window was left ajar for any brief moment they would force their

[1] Sarvatrotsrija Bheda-jnanam.

[2] All this happened in 1914. But India is now a changed country.

[3] A Panda is a Brahman priest attached to one of the temples. He runs a boarding-house where pilgrims visiting the place come and stay. Many of them are regular blood-suckers and make the life of the pilgrims miserable from the time they reach the railway station.

[4] The Arya Samaj was founded by Dayananda Saraswati. It aimed at a purification of Hindu religion and Hindu society by reverting to the pristine purity of the ancient times and of the original scriptures—the Vedas. The Arya Samaj does not believe in image-worship or in the caste system. In this respect it is similar to the Brahmo Samáj. The Arya Samaj has a large following in the Punjab and also in the United Provinces.

way in and carry away what they found or tear it into bits. We were not sorry to leave Muttra and from there we proceeded to Brindaban where on arrival we were surrounded by several Pandas who offered us board and lodging. To get out of their clutches we said that we wanted to go to the Gurukul institution. At once they put their fingers to their ears and said that no Hindu should go there. However, they were good enough to spare us their company.

Several miles away from Brindaban at a place called Kusum Sarobar, a number of Vaishnava ascetics were living in single-roomed cottages amid groves where deer and peacocks were roaming. It was indeed a beautiful spot—'meet nurse' for a religious mind. We visited them and were given a warm welcome and spent several days in their company. In that brotherhood was one Mouni Baba who had not spoken a word for ten years. The leader or guru of this colony was one Ramakrishnadas Babaji who was well-versed in Hindu philosophy. In his talks he maintained the position that the Vaishnavic doctrine of Dwaitadwaita[1] represented a further progress beyond the Adwaita doctrine of Monism of Shankaracharya. At that time Shankaracharya's doctrine represented to me the quintessence of Hindu philosophy—though I could not adapt my life to it and found the teaching of Ramakrishna and Vivekananda to be more practical—and I did not relish hearing Shankaracharya assailed by anyone. On the whole, I enjoyed my stay at Kusum-Sarobar and we left with a very high opinion of the ascetics there.

Coming to Benares we were welcomed at the Ramakrishna Mission's Muth by the late Swami Brahmananda

[1] This could perhaps be translated as 'Dualism beyond Monism'.

who knew my father and our family quite well. While I was there, a great deal of commotion was taking place at home. My parents who had waited long for my return were now feeling desperate. Something had to be done by my brothers and uncles. But what could they do? To inform the police did not appeal to them, for they were afraid that the police might harass more than they might help. So they betook themselves to a fortune-teller who had a reputation for honesty. This gentleman after taking counsel with the spirits announced that I was hale and hearty and was then at a place to the north-west of Calcutta, the name of which began with the letter B. It was immediately decided that that place must be Baidyanath[1] for there was an Ashrama there at the head of which was a well-known Yogi. No sooner was this decision made than one of my uncles was packed off there to get hold of me. But it proved to be a wild-goose chase for I was then at Benares.

After an exciting experience I turned up one fine morning quite unexpectedly. I was not repentant for having taken French leave, but I was somewhat crestfallen, not having found the guru I had wanted so much. A few days later I was in bed, down with typhoid—the price of pilgrimage and guru-hunting. Not even the soul can make the body defy the laws of health with impunity.

While I lay in bed the Great War broke out.

[1] Or rather Vaidyanath; in Bengali the pronunciation would be the same.

CHAPTER SEVEN

PRESIDENCY COLLEGE (2)

In spite of the political atmosphere of Calcutta and the propaganda carried on among the students by the terrorist-revolutionaries, I wonder how I would have developed politically, but for certain fortuitous circumstances. I often met, either in College or in the Hostel, several of those who—I learnt afterwards—were important men in the terrorist-revolutionary movement and who later were on the run. But I was never drawn towards them, not because I believed in non-violence as Mahatma Gandhi does, but because I was then living in a world of my own and held that the ultimate salvation of our people would come through process of national reconstruction. I must confess that the ideas of our group as to how we would be ultimately liberated were far from clear. In fact, it was sometimes seriously discussed whether it would not be a feasible plan to let the British manage the defence of India and reserve the civil administration to ourselves. But two things forced me to develop politically and to strike out an independent line for myself—the behaviour of Britishers in Calcutta and the Great War.

Since I left the P. E. School in January, 1909, I had had very little to do with Britishers. Between 1909 and 1913, only occasionally did I see a Britisher—perhaps some official visiting the school. In the town of Cuttack, too, I saw little of them, for they were few and lived in a remote part. But in Calcutta it was different. Every day while going to or returning from College, I had to pass through the quarter inhabited by

A SOLDIER IN MAKING
(Cadet in U.T.C., 1917)

them. Incidents in tram-cars occurred not infrequently. Britishers using these cars would be purposely rude and offensive to Indians in various ways. Sometimes they would put their feet up on the front-seats if they happened to be occupied by Indians, so that their shoes would touch the bodies of the latter. Many Indians—poor clerks going to office—would put up with the insult, but it was difficult for others to do so. I was not only sensitive by temperament but had been accustomed to a different treatment from my infancy. Often hot words would pass between Britishers and myself in the tram-cars. On rare occasions some Indian passengers would come to blows with them. On the streets the same thing happened. Britishers expected Indians to make way for them and if the latter did not do so, they were pushed aside by force or had their ears boxed. British Tommies were worse than civilians in this matter and among them the Gordon Highlanders had the worst reputation. In the railway trains it was sometimes difficult for an Indian to travel with self-respect, unless he was prepared to fight. The railway authorities or the police would not give the Indian passengers any legitimate protection, either because they were Britishers (or Anglo-Indians) themselves or because they were afraid of reporting against Britishers to the higher authorities. I remember an incident at Cuttack when I was a mere boy. One of my uncles had to return from the railway station because Britishers occupying the higher class compartments would not allow an Indian to come in. Occasionally we would hear stories of Indians in high position, including High Court judges, coming into conflict with Britishers in railway trains. Such stories had a knack of travelling far and wide.

Whenever I came across such an incident my dreams

would suffer a rude shock, and Shankaracharya's Doctrine of Maya would be shaken to its very foundations. It was quite impossible to persuade myself that to be insulted by a foreigner was an illusion that could be ignored. The situation would be aggravated if any Britishers on the College staff were rude or offensive to us. Unfortunately such instances were not rare.[1] I had some personal experience of them during my first year in College but they were not of a serious nature, though they were enough to stir up bitterness.

In conflicts of an inter-racial character the law was of no avail to Indians. The result was that after some time Indians, failing to secure any other remedy, began to hit back. On the streets, in the tram-cars, in the railway trains, Indians would no longer take things lying down.[2] The effect was instantaneous. Everywhere the Indian began to be treated with consideration. Then the word went round that the Englishman understands and respects physical force and nothing else. This phenomenon was the psychological basis of the terrorist-revolutionary movement—at least in Bengal.

Such experience as related above naturally roused my political consciousness but it was not enough to give a definite turn to my mental attitude. For that the shock of the Great War was necessary. As I lay in bed in July, 1914, glancing through the papers and somewhat disillusioned about Yogis and ascetics, I began to re-examine all my ideas and to revalue all the hitherto accepted values. Was it possible to divide a

[1] Before my time on several occasions English professors had been thrashed by the students. These stories were carefully chronicled and handed down from generation to generation.

[2] I knew a student in College, a good boxer, who would go out for his constitutional to the British quarter of the city and invite quarrels with Tommies.

nation's life into two compartments and hand over one of them to the foreigner, reserving the other to ourselves? Or was it incumbent on us to accept or reject life in its entirety? The answer that I gave myself was a perfectly clear one. If India was to be a modern civilised nation, she would have to pay the price and she would not by any means shirk the physical, the military, problem. Those who worked for the country's emancipation would have to be prepared to take charge of both the civil and military administration. Political freedom was indivisible and meant complete independence of foreign control and tutelage. The war had shown that a nation that did not possess military strength could not hope to preserve its independence.

After my recovery I resumed my usual activities and spent most of my time with my friends, but inwardly I had changed a great deal. Our group was developing rapidly, in number and in quality. One of the leading members, a promising doctor,[1] was sent to England for further studies so that on his return he could be of greater assistance to the group and greater service to the country. Everyone who could afford it contributed his mite towards his expenses and I gave a portion of my scholarship. Following this, another leading member accepted a commission in the Indian Medical Service, and it was hoped that he would thereby gain valuable experience and also lay by some money for future work.

After two years' hectic life my studies were in a hopeless condition. At the Intermediate Examination in 1915, though I was placed in the first division (which, by the way, was an easy affair), I was low down in the

[1] This experiment ended in failure for he married a French lady a settled in England and never returned to India.

list. I had a momentary feeling of remorse and then resolved to make good at the degree examination.

For my degree, I took the honours course in philosophy—a long cherished desire. I threw myself heart and soul into this work. For the first time in my College career I found interest in studies. But what I gained from this was quite different from what I had expected in my boyhood. At school I had expected that a study of philosophy would give me wisdom—knowledge about the fundamental questions of life and the world. I had possibly looked upon the study of philosophy as some sort of Yogic exercise and I was bound to be disappointed. I actually acquired not wisdom but intellectual discipline and a critical frame of mind. Western philosophy begins with doubt (some say it ends with doubt also). It regards everything with a critical eye, takes nothing on trust, and teaches us to argue logically and to detect fallacies. In other words, it emancipates the mind from preconceived notions. My first reaction to this was to question the truth of the Vedanta on which I had taken my stand so long. I began to write essays in defence of materialism, purely as an intellectual exercise. I soon came into conflict with the atmosphere of our group. It struck me for the first time that they were dogmatic in their views, taking certain things for granted, whereas a truly emancipated man should accept nothing without evidence and argument.

I was proceeding merrily with my studies when a sudden occurrence broke into my life. One morning in January, 1916, when I was in the College library I heard that a certain English professor had malhandled some students belonging to our year. On enquiry it appeared that some of our class-mates were walking along the corridor adjoining Mr O.'s lecture-room, when

Mr O., feeling annoyed at the disturbance, rushed out of the room and violently pushed back a number of students who were in the front row. We had a system of class-representatives whom the Principal[1] consulted on general matters and I was the representative of my class. I immediately took the matter up with the Principal and suggested among other things that Mr O. should apologise to the students whom he had insulted. The Principal said that since Mr O. was a member of the Indian Educational Service, he could not coerce him into doing that. He said further that Mr O. had not malhandled any students or used force against them—but had simply "taken them by the arm" which did not amount to an insult. We were naturally not satisfied and the next day there was a general strike of all the students. The Principal resorted to all sorts of coercive and diplomatic measures in order to break the strike, but to no avail. Even the Moulvi Sahib's efforts to wean away the Muslim students ended in failure. Likewise the appeals of popular professors like Sir P. C. Ray and Dr D. N. Mullick fell flat. Among other disciplinary measures, the Principal levied a general fine on all the absentee students.

A successful strike in the Presidency College was a source of great excitement throughout the city. The strike contagion began to spread, and the authorities began to get nervous. One of my professors who was rather fond of me was afraid that I would land myself in trouble being one of the strike-leaders. He took me aside and quietly asked me if I realised what I was in for. I said that I was—whereupon he said that he would say nothing more. However, at the end of the second day's strike, pressure was brought to bear on Mr O. He

[1] Mr H. R. J. (deceased)

sent for the students' representatives and settled the dispute amicably with them, a formula honourable to both parties having been devised in the meantime.

The next day the lectures were held and the students assembled in an atmosphere of 'forgive and forget'. It was naturally expected that after the settlement the Principal would withdraw the penal measures he had adopted during the strike, but they were disappointed. He would not budge an inch—the fine would have to be paid unless a student pleaded poverty. All appeals made by the students as well as by the professors proved to be unavailing. The fine rankled in the minds of the students, but nothing could be done.

About a month later a similar incident came like a bolt from the blue. The report went out that Mr O. had again malhandled a student—but this time it was a student of the first year. What were the students to do? Constitutional protests like strikes would simply provoke disciplinary measures and appeals to the Principal would be futile. Some students therefore decided to take the law into their own hands. The result was that Mr O. was subjected to the argument of force and in the process was beaten black and blue. From the newspaper office to Government House everywhere there was wild commotion.

It was alleged at the time that the students had attacked Mr O. from behind and thrown him down the stairs. This allegation is entirely false. Mr O. did receive one solitary stroke from behind, but that was of no account. His assailants—those who felled him—were all in front of him and on the same level with him. Being an eye witness myself I can assert this without fear of contradiction. It is necessary that this point should be made clear in fairness to the students.

Immediately after this the Government of Bengal issued a communique ordering the College to be closed and appointing a Committee of Enquiry to go into the continued disturbances in that institution. The temper of the Government was naturally very high and it was freely rumoured that the Government would not hesitate to close down the College for good. No doubt the Government would have given the fullest support to the staff as against the students. But as ill-luck would have it, the Principal fell out with the Government over the official communique. As the Government orders were issued over his head, he felt that his *amour propre* had been hurt and his prestige damaged. He called on the Honourable Member in charge of Education and made a scene at his place. The next day another official communique was issued saying that the Principal[1] was placed under suspension for "gross personal insult" to the Honourable Member.

But before power could slip out of his hands the Principal acted. He sent for all those students who were in his black list including myself. To me he said—or rather snarled—in unforgettable words, "Bose, you are the most troublesome man in the College. I suspend you." I said "Thank you," and went home. Shankaracharya's Maya lay dead as a door nail.

Soon after the Governing Body met and confirmed the Principal's order. I was expelled from the Presidency College. I appealed to the University for per-

[1] Subsequently, the Principal was reinstated, probably after he had made amends and then he retired for good. Here I must say in fairness to him that he was very popular with the students for protecting them against police persecution on several occasions. On the present occasion he probably lost his head and could not decide whether he should side entirely with the authorities or with the students. If he had done either, he would have had at least one party to side with him.

mission to study in some other college. That was refused. So I was virtually rusticated from the University.

What was to be done? Some politicians comforted me by saying that the Principal's orders were *ultra vires* since the Committee of Enquiry had taken over all his powers. All eyes were turned to the Committee.

The Committee was presided over by Sir Asutosh Mukherji, former Vice-Chancellor and Judge of the High Court. Naturally we expected justice. I was one of those who had to represent the students' case. I was asked a straight question—Whether I considered the assault on Mr O. to be justified. My reply was that though the assault was not justified, the students had acted under great provocation. And I then proceeded to narrate seriatim the misdeeds of the Britishers in Presidency College during the last few years. It was a heavy indictment, but wiseacres thought that by not unconditionally condemning the assault on Mr O. I had ruined my own case. I felt, however, that I had done the right thing regardless of its effect on me.

I lingered on in Calcutta hoping against hope that something favourable would turn up. The Committee submitted its report and there was hardly a word in favour of the students. Mine was the only name singled out for mention—so my fate was sealed.

Meanwhile the political atmosphere in Calcutta grew from bad to worse. Wholesale arrests were made, and among the latest victims were some expelled students of the Presidency College. My elder brothers were alarmed and held a hurried consultation. The consensus of opinion was that to stay in Calcutta without any ostensible vocation was extremely risky. I should, therefore, be packed off to a quiet corner like Cuttack where there was comparative safety.

Lying on the bunk in the train at night I reviewed the events of the last few months. My educational career was at an end, and my future was dark and uncertain. But I was not sorry—there was not a trace of regret in my mind for what I had done. I had rather a feeling of supreme satisfaction, of joy that I had done the right thing, that I had stood up for our honour and self-respect and had sacrificed myself for a noble cause. After all, what is life without renunciation, I told myself. And I went to sleep.

Little did I then realise the inner significance of the tragic events of 1916. My Principal had expelled me, but he had made my future career. I had established a precedent for myself from which I could not easily depart in future. I had stood up with courage and composure in a crisis and fulfilled my duty. I had developed self-confidence as well as initiative, which was to stand me in good stead in future. I had a foretaste of leadership—though in a very restricted sphere—and of the martyrdom that it involves. In short, I had acquired character and could face the future with equanimity.

CHAPTER EIGHT

MY STUDIES RESUMED

It was the end of March, 1916, when I came down to Cuttack as a rusticated student. Fortunately, no stigma attached to that appellation. By students everywhere I was regarded with sympathy tinged with respect, because I had stood up for their cause. There was no change whatsoever in the attitude of my parents and, strange to say, my father never put one question to me about the events in College or my part therein. My elder brothers in Calcutta had sympathised with me in my tribulations believing that I had done the right thing in the circumstances that I had to face. My parents' attitude, as far as I could judge from their behaviour in spite of their reserve, seemed to be that I had to suffer for being the spokesman of the students. It was a great relief to know that I had the sympathy of those with whom I had to spend my days and nights and that they did not think ill of me because I had been sent down.

Thus my relations with my family did not suffer a set-back, but rather improved. The same could not be said of the group. Throughout the exciting events of January and February I had not taken counsel with them and had acted entirely on my own initiative. Later on I gathered that they did not quite approve of what I had done and would have liked to see me avoid a direct conflict with the powers that be. When I decided to leave Calcutta I did not so much as inform them, though previously I had spent days and nights in their company, joining in their plans for the future. By this time the group had become a well-knit organisation. Most of the important members in Calcutta belonging to different institutions used to live in one boarding-house, where every afternoon those living at home or in other hostels would assemble for discussion and exchange of ideas. The group was bringing out for private circulation a manuscript journal as its organ. Regular lessons used to be given to educate the members in different subjects, and since emphasis was laid on moral and religious training it was but natural that 'Gita' classes should form a regular feature of the afternoon gatherings.

It will be easily realised that after the recent happenings, mentally I was not the same man as when I left home and comfort two years ago to find a guru for myself. The change came somewhat suddenly—like a storm—and turned everything upside down. But long before the storm broke, a silent change had been going on within me of which I was unconscious at the time. Firstly, I was being pulled in the direction of social service. Secondly, in spite of all my eccentricities, I was acquiring moral stamina. Consequently, when I was faced with a sudden crisis which put to the test my sense of social duty, I was not found wanting. Without a tremor I took my stand and gladly faced the consequences. Shyness and diffidence vanished into thin air.

What was I to do now? I could not continue my studies because I did not know where and when I would have to begin again. The expulsion being for an indefinite period amounted to a sentence for life, and there was no certainty that the University authorities would relent after a time and permit me to resume my studies. I sounded my parents as to whether they would send me abroad to study, but my father set his face against the idea. He was definitely of opinion that I should have the blot on my escutcheon removed before I could think of going abroad. That meant taking my degree from the Calcutta University first.

I had therefore to hold my soul in patience till the University authorities would think of reconsidering their orders, and meanwhile I had to fill my time somehow. Putting my books aside, I took to social service with passionate zeal. In those days epidemics like cholera and smallpox were of frequent occurrence in Orissa. Most people were too poor to afford a doctor and, even when they could do so, there was the further difficulty of finding nurses. It would sometimes happen that if cholera broke out in a hostel or boarding-house, the inmates would clear off bag and baggage, leaving the victims to their fate. There is no reason to be surprised at this, because prior to the introduction of saline injection treatment following the researches of Leonard Rogers, cholera was a most fatal disease, and in addition highly contagious. Fortunately, there was a group among the students, consisting partly of my old friends, who would go out to different parts of the city and do voluntary nursing. I readily joined them. We concentrated on such fell diseases as cholera and smallpox, but our services were available for other diseases as well. We also did duty in the cholera ward of the local Civil Hospital, for there were no trained nurses there and nursing was left in the hands of ignorant and dirty sweepers. In spite of the dire lack of adequate nursing, the cholera mortality in the hospital was much lower than in the village we had visited two years ago with a box of homoeopathic medicine and under the leadership of a half-doctor. The fact is that saline injections worked like magic and, when they were administered at an early state of the disease, there was eighty per cent chance of recovery.

Nursing cholera patients we enjoyed greatly, especially when we found that several patients were thereby saved from the jaws of death. But in the matter of taking precautions, I was criminally negligent. I never cared to disinfect my clothes when I returned home and, of course, I did not volunteer information to anybody as to where I had been. I wonder that during all the months that I had been doing nursing I did not carry infection to other people or get infected myself.

With cholera patients I never had a feeling of repulsion even when I had to handle soiled clothes, but I could not say the same of smallpox in an advanced stage of suppuration. It required all my strength of mind to force me to attend such a patient. However, as a schooling, this sort of voluntary work had its value and I did not shirk it.

Nursing brought in other allied problems. What about those who died in spite of doctoring and nursing? There was no association for taking charge of the dead bodies and cremating them in the proper manner. In the case of unclaimed bodies, the municipal sweepers would come and dispose of them as they liked. But who would relish the idea of having his body labelled as unclaimed after his death? The nurses, therefore, were often called upon to function as undertakers. According to the Indian custom we would have to carry the dead body ourselves to the cremation ground and perform the funeral rites. The problem was comparatively simple when the dead person had well-to-do relatives and only needed volunteers. But there were cases when there was no money available and we had to send the hat round for meeting the expenses of cremation. Apart from cases which volunteers had nursed, there were other cases where outside physical help was needed to perform the funeral rites and we had to minister in such cases as well.

Interesting and useful though nursing was, it could not fill all my time. Moreover, nursing was but an expedient; it was not a permanent remedy for any of our national ills. In our group we had always criticised the Ramakrishna Mission for concentrating on hospitals and flood and famine relief and neglecting nation-building work of a permanent nature, and I had no desire to repeat their mistake. Consequently, I tried my hand at youth organisation. I got together a large number of youths and we started an organisation with different departments for their physical, intellectual, and moral advancement. This work went on pretty well while I was there. About this time I was brought face to face with the problem of untouchability. In a students' hostel which was one of our favourite haunts there was a Santal student called Majhi. The Santals are generally looked upon as an inferior caste, but the students who were broadminded did not mind that, and Majhi was welcomed as a boarder. Things went on all right for a time. One day a personal servant of one of the boarders somehow came to know that Majhi was a Santal and he tried to stir up trouble by calling upon the other servants to refuse to work in the hostel if Majhi did not leave. Fortunately nobody was in a mood to listen to his demand and the trouble was nipped in the bud. What struck me at the time was that the really higher castes, who could have objected, never so much as thought of the case of the Santal student—whereas the servant who himself belonged to a comparatively low caste appeared highly indignant.

Soon after this incident Majhi fell ill with typhoid and we made it a point to nurse him with extra care and consideration. In this, to my great surprise and joy, my mother joined me.

To fill the gaps in my time I went out on excursions with friends to different places of religious or historical interest. Life in the open with plenty of walking was good for the health and it gave opportunities for that intimate communion with other souls which is never possible within the four walls of a room. Moreover, it helped me to keep away from home where I had nothing particular to do, because individualistic Yoga had no longer any attraction for me and the study of text-books did not interest me. I now tried an experiment in using our religious festivals for developing our group life. From the earliest times the important religious ceremonies have been festivals in which the whole of society participates. Take the Durga Poojah in a village in Bengal. Though the religious part of the Poojah lasts only five days, work in connection with it lasts several weeks. During this period practically every caste or profession in the village is needed for some work or other in connection with the Poojah. Thus, though the Poojah may be performed in one home, the whole village participates in the festivity and also profits financially from it. In my infancy in our village home a drama used to be staged at the end of the Poojah which the whole village would enjoy. During the last fifty years, owing to the gradual impoverishment of the country and migration from the villages, these religious festivals have been considerably reduced and in some cases have ceased altogether. This has affected the circulation of money within the village economy and on the social side has made life dull and drab.

There is another form of religious festivity in which the community participates even more directly. In such cases the Poojah is performed not in a home but in some public hall and the expenses are borne not by one family, but by the community. These festivals, called Baroari Poojah,[1] have also been gradually going out of existence. So in 1917 we decided to organise such a Poojah. On the social side it was a great success and it was therefore repeated in the following years.

During this period, on the mental side I remember to have made a distinct progress in one respect, that of the practice of self-analysis.[2] This is a practice which I have regularly indulged in ever since and have benefited greatly thereby. It consists in throwing a powerful searchlight on your own mind with a view to knowing yourself better. Usually before going to sleep or in the early morning I would spend some time over this. This analysis would be of two kinds—analysis of myself as I was at that time and analysis of my whole life. From the former I would get to know more about my hidden desires and impulses, ideals and aspirations. From the latter I would begin to comprehend my life better, to view it from the evolutionary standpoint, to understand how in the past I had been struggling to fulfil myself, to realise my errors of the past and thereby draw conclusions for the future.

I had not practised self-analysis long before I made two discoveries, both important for myself. Firstly, I knew very little about my own mind till then, that there were ignoble impulses within me which masqueraded

[1] During the last ten years Baroari Poojah has once again become extremely popular in Calcutta. Physical display, exhibitions, etc. are organised in connection with these Poojahs.

[2] I hit upon this method quite empirically in my effort to master my own mind. At that time I did not know anything about psycho-analysis.

under a more presentable exterior. Secondly, the moment I put my finger on something ignoble or unworthy within me, I half-conquered it. Weaknesses of the mind, unlike diseases of the body, flourished only when they were not detected. When they were found out, they had a tendency to take to their heels.[1]

One of the immediate uses I made of self-analysis was in ridding myself of certain disturbing dreams. I had fought against such dreams in my earlier life with some measure of success, but as I gradually improved my method of analysis, I got even better results. The earliest dreams of an unpleasant character were those of snakes, wild animals, etc. In order to rid myself of snake-dreams, I would sit down at night before going to sleep and picture myself in a closed room full of poisonous snakes and repeat to myself—'I am not afraid of being bitten; I am not afraid of death'. While thinking hard in this way I would doze off to sleep. After I practised in this way for a few days I noticed a change. At first the snakes appeared in my dreams but without frightening me. Then they dropped off altogether. Dreams of other wild animals were similarly dealt with. Since then I have had no trouble at all.

About the time I was expelled from College I began to have dreams of house-searches and arrests. Undoubtedly they were a reflection of my subconscious thoughts and hidden anxieties. But a few days' exercise cured me altogether. I had only to picture to myself house-searches and arrests going on without disturbing me and to repeat to myself that I was not upset in any way. Another class of dreams which occasionally

[1] Later on when I took up the study of psychology I learnt that a mental conflict was cured immediately the sufferer understood its origin or cause through psycho-analysis.

disturbed me, though not to the same extent, was about examinations for which I was not prepared or in which I fared badly. To tackle such dreams I had to repeat to myself that I was fully prepared for the examination and was sure of doing well. I know of people who are troubled by such dreams till late in life, and sometimes get into an awful fright in their dreams. For such people a more prolonged exercise may be necessary, but relief is sure to come if they persist. If a particular class of dreams appears to be persistent, a closer analysis should be made of them with a view to discovering their composition.

The dreams most difficult to get rid of are those about sex. This is because sex is one of the most powerful instincts in man and because there is a periodicity in sex-urge which occasions such dreams at certain intervals. Nevertheless, it is possible to obtain at least partial relief. That, at any rate, has been my experience. The method would be to picture before the mind the particular form that excites one in his dreams and to repeat to himself that it does not excite him any longer—that he has conquered lust. For instance, if it is the case of a man being excited by a woman, the best course would be for him to picture that form before his mind as the form of his mother or sister. One is likely to get discouraged in his fight with sex-dreams unless he remembers that there is a periodicity in sex-urge which does not apply to other instincts and that the sex-instinct can be conquered or sublimated only gradually.

To continue our narrative, I returned to Calcutta after a year's absence in order to try my luck with the University authorities once again. It was a difficult job, but the key to the situation was with Sir Asutosh Mukherji, the virtual dictator of the University. If he willed it, the penal order could be withdrawn. While waiting for the matter to come up, I grew restless and looked out for a suitable outlet for my energy. Just then the campaign for recruitment to the 49th Bengalees was going on. I attended a recruiting meeting at the University Institute and felt greatly interested. The next day I quietly went to the office in Beadon Street where recruits were medically examined and offered myself for recruitment. Army medical examinations are always nasty and they show no consideration for any sense of shame. I went through it without flinching. I was sure that I would pass all the other tests, but I was nervous about my eyesight which was defective. I implored the I.M.S. officer, who happened to be an Indian, to pass me as fit, but he regretted that for an eye examination I would have to go to another officer. There is a saying in Bengali—'it gets dark just where there is a fear of a tiger appearing'—and so it happened in this case. This officer, one Major Cook I think, happened to be very particular about eye-sight and, though I had passed every other test, he disqualified me. Heartbroken I returned home.

I was informed that the University authorities would probably be amenable, but that I would have to find a College where I could be admitted if the University had no objection. The Bangabasi College offered to take me in, but there was no provision there for the honours course in philosophy. So I decided to approach the Scottish Church College. One fine morning without any introduction whatsoever I went straight to the Principal of that College, Dr Urquhart, and told him that I was an expelled student, but that the University was going to lift the ban, and I wanted to study for the honours course in philosophy in his College. He was evidently favourably impressed, for he agreed to admit me, provided the Principal of the Presidency College did not stand in the way. I would have to get a note from him to the effect that he had no objection to my admission into the Scottish Church College. That was not an easy task for me. My second brother, Sjt. Sarat Chandra Bose, who was my guardian in Calcutta, however, offered to do this for me and he interviewed the new Principal.[1] Mr W., he told me, was quite tractable on this point but he wanted me to call on him once. I went and was put through a searching cross examination about the events of the previous year. At the end he wound up by saying he was concerned more with the future than the past and would not object to my going to some other institution. That was all that I wanted, I had no desire to go back to the Presidency College.

Once admitted, I took to my studies with zeal and devotion. I had lost two years and when I joined the third year class again in July, 1917, my class-mates had taken their B.A. and were studying for their M.A. degree. At College I led a quiet life. There was no possibility of any friction with the authorities with such a tactful and considerate man as Dr Urquhart as Principal. He was himself a philosophy man and lectured on that subject, besides giving Bible lessons. His Bible lessons were very interesting and, for the first time, the Bible did not bore me. It was such a welcome change from the Bible lessons in the P. E. School. Life was humdrum in College except for the fact that I took part in the activities of the College Societies, especially the Philosophical Society. But I soon found something to add some spice to my daily life.

The Government had agreed to start a University

[1] Mr W.

unit in the India Defence Force—India's Territorial Army—and recruiting was going on for this unit, a double company. The physical tests would not be so stiff as in the regular army tests, especially in the matter of vision. So there was a chance of my getting in. This experiment was being sponsored on the Indian side by the late Dr Suresh Chandra Sarvadhikari,[1] the famous Calcutta surgeon, whose zeal for providing military training for Bengalees was unbounded. I was not disappointed this time. Our training began at the Calcutta Maidan in mufti and the officers and instructors were provided by the Lincolns Regiment in Fort William. It was a motley crowd that assembled there the first day to answer the roll-call. Some in dhoti (Bengalee style), some in shorts (semi-military style), some in trousers (civilian style), some bareheaded, some in turbans, some with hats, and so on. It did not look as if soldiers could be made out of them. But the entire aspect changed when two months later we shifted to the vicinity of the Fort, got into military uniform, pitched our tents, and began drilling with our rifles. We had camp life for four months and enjoyed it thoroughly. Part of it was spent at Belghurriah about twelve miles from Calcutta

[1] Dr Sarvadhikari, Dr S. K. Mullick (now dead) and some others were pioneers of the movement to persuade the Government to admit Bengalees into the Army. During the war, when the Government was hard up in the matter of man-power, they were successful. Bengalees were first allowed to join the Ambulance Corps and were sent to Mesopotamia. As they had a very good record there, they were admitted into the regular army and the 49th Bengalees was then started. Bengalees were also admitted into the Indian Territorial Force and the University Infantry was the university section of that force. The University Infantry is now a permanent corps but the Bengalee units in the regular army were disbanded at the end of the war. In 1916 I met a demobilised officer of the Bengal Ambulance Corps who had been present at the siege of Kut-el-Amara and thereafter was a prisoner of war in Turkey. I was greatly excited by his tales of adventure and wanted to join the army.

where we had our musketry practice at the rifle range. What a change it was from sitting at the feet of anchorites to obtain knowledge about God, to standing with a rifle on my shoulder taking orders from a British army officer!

We did not see any active service nor did we have any real adventure. Nevertheless we were enthusiastic over our camp-life. There is no doubt that it engendered real *esprit de corps*, though we had never experienced anything like military life before. Besides our parade we had recreation of all sorts—official and unofficial—and sports as well. Towards the end of our training we had mock-fights in the dark which were interesting and exciting to a degree. The company had its comic figures and many were the jokes we would have at their expense. At an early stage they were put in a separate squad, called the 'Awkward Squad'. But as they improved, they were drafted into the regular platoons. Jack Johnson,[1] however, refused to change and till the last he stood out as a unique personality and had to be tolerated even by the Officer Commanding.

Our O.C., Captain Gray, was a character. He was a ranker, which meant much, considering the conservative traditions of the British Army. It would be difficult to find a better instructor than he. A rough Scotsman with a gruff voice, on the parade-ground he always wore a scowl on his face. But he had a heart of gold. He always meant well and his men knew it and therefore liked him, despite his brusque manners. For Captain Gray we will do anything—that is how we felt at the time. When he joined our Company, the staff officers in Fort William were of opinion that we would be utter failures as soldiers. Captain Gray showed that their

[1] That was his nickname.

estimate was wrong. The fact is that, being all educated men, we picked up very soon. What ordinary soldiers would take months to learn we would master in so many weeks. After three weeks' musketry training there was a shooting competition between our men and our instructors, and the latter were beaten hollow. Our instructors refused to believe at first that our men had never handled rifles before. I remember asking our platoon-instructor one day to tell me frankly what he thought of us as soldiers. He said that on parade we were quite smart but that our fighting stamina could be tested only during active service. Our O.C. was satisfied with our turn-out, at least he said so when we broke up, and he felt proud when the military secretary to the Governor complimented us on our parade, the day we furnished the guard-of-honour to His Excellency at the Calcutta University Convocation. His satisfaction was even greater when we did well at the Proclamation Parade on New Year's Day.

I wonder how much I must have changed from those days when I could find pleasure in soldiering. Not only was there no sign of maladaptation to my new environment but I found a positive pleasure in it. This training gave me something which I needed or which I lacked. The feeling of strength and of self-confidence grew still further. As soldiers we had certain rights which as Indians we did not possess. To us as Indians, Fort William was out of bounds, but as soldiers we had right of entry there, and as a matter of fact the first day we marched into Fort William to bring our rifles, we experienced a queer feeling of satisfaction, as if we were taking possession of something to which we had an inherent right but of which we had been unjustly deprived. The route-marches in the city and elsewhere we enjoyed, probably because it gave us a sense of importance. We could snap our fingers at the police and other agents of the Government by whom we were in the habit of being harassed or terrorised.

The third year in College was given up to soldiering and the excitement connected therewith. Only in my fourth year[1] did I commence my studies in right earnest. At the B.A. Examination in 1919 I did well, but not up to my expectations. I got first-class honours in philosophy but was placed second in order of merit. For my M.A. course I did not want to continue philosophy. As I have remarked before, I was to some extent disillusioned about philosophy. While it developed the critical faculty, provoked scepticism, and fostered intellectual discipline, it did not solve any of the fundamental problems for me. My problems could be solved only by myself. Besides this consideration there was another factor at work. I myself had changed considerably during the last three years. I decided therefore to study experimental psychology for my M.A. examination. It was a comparatively new science I found absorbing, but I was not destined to continue it for more than a few months.

One evening, when my father was in Calcutta, he suddenly sent for me. I found him closeted with my second brother, Sarat. He asked me if I would like to go to England to study for the Indian Civil Service. If I agreed I should start as soon as possible. I was given twenty-four hours to make up my mind.

It was an utter surprise to me. I took counsel with

[1] In the Indian Universities after the 1st and 2nd year comes the Intermediate Examination. After the 3rd and 4th year comes the B.A. or B.Sc. Examination and after the 5th and 6th year comes the M.A. or M.Sc. Examination.

myself and, within a few hours, made up my mind to go. All my plans about researches in psychology were put aside. How often, I wondered, were my carefully laid plans going to be shattered by the superior force of circumstances. I was not so sorry to part company with psychology, but what about joining the Indian Civil Service and accepting a job under the British Government? I had not thought of that even in my dreams. I persuaded myself, however, that I could never pass the I.C.S. examination at such short notice, for by the time I reached England and settled down to study, barely eight months would be left and I had but one chance, in view of my age. If, however, I managed to get through, there would be plenty of time to consider what I should do.

I had to leave at a week's notice. A berth was somehow secured in a boat going all the way by sea. But the difficulty was about my passport. There one was left to the tender mercies of the C.I.D., especially in a province like Bengal. And from the police point of view, my antecedents were certainly not irreproachable. Through the good offices of a high police official who was a distant relative of mine, I was introduced to police headquarters and within six days my passport was forthcoming. A marvel indeed!

Once again I had done things off my own bat. When I consulted the group regarding my proposed journey to England, they threw cold water on the project. One of the most promising members who had been to England had married and settled down there and did not think of returning. It was dangerous to try another experiment. But I was adamant. What did it matter if one member had gone astray? It did not follow that others would do the same, so I argued. My relations with the group had been growing increasingly lukewarm for some time past, and I had joined the University infantry without consulting them. But this was the limit. Though we did not say so, we felt that we had come to the parting of the ways, since I was determined to strike out a line for myself.

Then I visited the Provincial Advisor for studies in England, himself a product of Cambridge and a Professor of the Presidency College. He knew me by sight and naturally did not have a high opinion of an expelled student. As soon as he heard that I intended to sit for the I.C.S. examination the next year, he summoned up all his powers of dissuasion. I had no chance whatsoever against the 'tip-toppers' from Oxford and Cambridge; why was I going to throw away ten thousand rupees? That was the burden of his homily. Realising the force of his argument and unable to find an answer to his question, I simply said, "My father wants me to throw away the ten thousand rupees." Then seeing that he would do nothing to help me secure admission to Cambridge, I left him.

Relying entirely on my own resources and determined to try my luck in England, I set sail on the 15th September, 1919.

Like Father—Like Son
JANAKINATH—SUBHAS CHANDRA

CHAPTER NINE

AT CAMBRIDGE

When I left India the Jallianwalla Bagh massacre at Amritsar had already taken place. But hardly any news of it had travelled outside the Punjab. Punjab was under martial law and there was a strict censorship on all news sent out from that province. As a consequence, we had heard only vague rumours of some terrible happenings at Lahore and Amritsar. One of my brothers who was then working at Simla brought us some news—or rather rumours—about the Punjab happenings and also about the Anglo-Afghan war in which the Afghans had got the better of the British. But on the whole the public were ignorant of what had been going on in the north-west, and I sailed for Europe in a complacent mood.

On the boat we found quite a number of Indian passengers, mostly students. Accordingly we considered it advisable to take a separate table where we would feel more at home. Our table was presided over by an elderly and estimable lady, the wife of a deceased Indian Civil Servant. The majority of the passengers were Britishers of the sub-burnt snobbish type. Association with them was hardly possible—so we Indians kept mostly to ourselves. Occasionally there would be friction between an Indian passenger and a Britisher over some thing or other, and though nothing very serious took place by the time we reached England, we all had a feeling of resentment at the supercilious attitude of the Britisher towards Indians. One interesting discovery I made during the voyage—Anglo-Indians develop a love for India and the Indian people when they are out of India. In the boat there were a few Anglo-Indian passengers. The nearer we came to Europe, the more home-sick—I mean 'India-sick'—they became. In England Anglo-Indians cannot pass themselves off as Englishmen. They have, moreover, no home there, no associations, no contacts. It is, therefore, inevitable that the farther they go from India, the closer they should feel drawn towards her.

I do not think that we could have chosen a slower boat than the *City of Calcutta*. She was scheduled to reach Tilbury in 30 days but actually took a week more. That was because she was held up at Suez for want of coal, owing to the coal-strike in England. Our only consolation was that we called at a number of ports on our way. To make life on board for five weeks somewhat bearable, we had to fall back on that spice of life, humour. One fellow-passenger had been ordered by his wife not to touch beef. By another passenger he was tricked into taking 'copta curry' of beef—which he thoroughly enjoyed—under the impression that it was mutton 'copta curry'. Great was his remorse when he discovered his mistake after twelve hours. Another passenger had orders from his fiancee to write a letter every day. He spent his time reciting love-poems and talking about her. Whether we liked it or not, we had to listen. He was beside himself with joy when one day I remarked in reply to his importunity that his fiancee had Grecian features.

Even the longest day has its end; so we did reach Tilbury after all. It was wet and cloudy—typical London weather. But there was plenty of excitement to make us oblivious of outside nature. When I first went down into a tube-station, I enjoyed the experience, for it was something new.

The next morning I began exploring. I called at the office of the Adviser to Indian students at Cromwell Road. He was very nice to me, gave me plenty of advice, but added that so far as admission to Cambridge was concerned, there was nothing doing. There by chance I met some Indian students from Cambridge. One of them strongly advised me to proceed straight to Cambridge and try my luck there, instead of wasting my time at Cromwell Road. I agreed, and the next day I was at Cambridge. Some students from Orissa, whom I had known slightly before, lent me a helping hand. One[1] of them who belonged to Fitzwilliam Hall took me to Mr Reddaway, the Censor, and introduced me to him. Mr Reddaway was exceedingly kind and sympathetic, gave me a patient hearing, and at the end wound up by saying that he would admit me straight away. The problem of admission settled, the next question was about the current term which had begun two weeks ago. If I lost that term then I would probably have to spend nearly a year more in order to qualify for a degree. Otherwise, I would take my degree by June, 1921. On this point also Mr Reddaway was accommodating beyond my expectation. He made use of the coal-strike and of my military service in order to persuade the University authorities to stretch a point in my favour. He succeeded, and the result was that I did not lose that term. Without Mr Reddaway I do not know what I would have done in England.

I reached London about the 25th October and it was the first week of November before I could settle down to work at Cambridge. I had an unusually large

[1] S. M. D.

number of lectures to attend—part of them for the Mental and Moral Sciences Tripos and the rest for the Civil Service Examination. Outside my lecture hours I had to study as hard as I could. There was no question of any enjoyment for me, besides what I could get from hard work. I was to appear under the old Civil Service Regulations which necessitated my taking up eight or nine different subjects, some of which I had to study for the first time. My subjects were as follows: English Composition, Sanskrit, Philosophy, English Law, Political Science, Modern European History, English History, Economics, Geography. Over and above studying these subjects, I had to do surveying and map-making (Cartography) for the Geography paper and to learn something of French in connection with the Modern History paper.

The work for the Mental and Moral Sciences Tripos was more interesting but I could not devote much time to it, beyond attending the lectures. Among my lecturers were Prof. Sorley (Ethics), Prof. Myers (Psychology), and Prof. McTaggart (Metaphysics). During the first three terms I devoted practically my whole time to preparing for the Civil Service Examination. In the way of recreation, I attended the meetings of the Indian Majlis and the Union Society.

Cambridge after the war was conservative. Oxford was much the same but was beginning to go liberal. One could judge of the prevailing atmosphere from the fact that pacifists, socialists, conscientious objectors, and the like could not easily address a public meeting at Cambridge. The undergraduates would generally come and break up the meetings and 'rag' the lecturer by throwing bags of flour at him or giving him a ducking in the river. 'Ragging' was of course a legitimate recreation for the undergraduates there and I heartily approved of it. But breaking up meetings simply because the speaker represented a different ideology did not appeal to me.

What greatly impressed an outsider like myself was the measures of freedom allowed to the students, and the general esteem in which they were held by all and sundry. This undoubtedly had a very wholesome effect on their character. What a change, I thought, from a police-ridden city like Calcutta where every student was looked upon as a potential revolutionary and suspect! And living in the atmosphere of Cambridge, it was difficult to imagine the incidents in the Calcutta Presidency College—professors maltreating students—for there it was the professors who ran the risk of being maltreated by the undergraduates. In fact, unpopular dons were occasionally 'ragged' by the undergrads and their rooms raided by the latter though in a friendly way, for later on they were compensated for any damage done. Even when a ragging was going on in the streets of Cambridge, causing damage to public property, the police would behave with remarkable restraint, a thing quite impossible in India.

Apart from the measure of freedom enjoyed by the students, which would naturally appeal more to me than to British students born and brought up in a free atmosphere, the consideration and esteem with which they were treated everywhere was very striking. Even a fresher coming up for the first time would at once get the impression that a high standard of character and behaviour was expected of him, and he would be bound to react favourably. This consideration shown towards the undergraduates was not confined to Cambridge but existed to some extent all over the country. In the trains when one was questioned and replied that he was at Cambridge (or Oxford), the attitude of the questioner would change at once. He would become friendly—or shall I say more respectful? This was my personal experience. If there is an element of snobbishness in those who go up to Cambridge or Oxford, I certainly do not hold a brief for it. But, having been brought up in a police-ridden atmosphere, it is my firm conviction that there is a lot to be said in favour of allowing students and young men more freedom and treating them with consideration as if they were responsible citizens.

I remember an incident when I was a College student in Calcutta. I was then awfully fond of buying new books. If I set my heart on a book in a shop-window, I would not rest till I possessed it. I would feel so restless till I got the book that I had to buy it before I returned home. One day I went to one of the biggest shops in College Street and asked for a book on philosophy, on which I was very keen at the time. The price was announced and I found that I was short by a few rupees. I requested the manager to let me have the book and promised to bring the balance the next day. He replied that that was not possible, I would have to pay the full price down first. I was not only disappointed at failing to get the book but was extremely hurt because I was distrusted in this way.[1] It was therefore such a relief to find that you could walk into any shop in Cambridge and order anything you liked without having to bother about payment on the spot.

There is another thing which drew my admiration—the debates at the Union Society's meetings. The whole

[1] I know that things have changed now.

atmosphere was so exhilarating. There was perfect freedom to talk what you liked or attack whomsoever you wished. Prominent members of Parliament and sometimes members of the Cabinet took part in these debates in a spirit of perfect equality and would, of course, come in for slashing criticism not unmixed with invective at times. Once Horatio Bottomley, M. P. was taking part in a debate. He was warned by an oppositionist speaker—"There are more things in heaven and earth, Horatio, than your John Bull dreams of."

Sparkling bits of humour would enliven the proceedings. During the course of a debate on Ireland a pro-Irish speaker, while exposing the real character of the Government, referred to the "forces of law and order on one side and of Bonar Law and disorder on the other."

Among the guests at these debates, besides well-known parliamentary figures, there were also those who were on the threshold of a public career. I remember, for instance, that Dr Hugh Dalton was often present at these debates. He was a prospective M. P. nursing some constituency at the time. Sir Oswald Mosely, then a Left Wing Liberal (or Labourite) participated in a debate on India. He vehemently denounced[1] the policy of Dyer and O'dwyer and raised a storm in British circles by his remark that the events in Amritsar in 1919 were the expression of racial hatred. Sir John Simon and Mr Clynes once came to plead the miners' cause before the Cambridge public at Guildhall. The undergrads turned up with the object of giving them a hot time. Sir John Simon had to run the gauntlet, but when Mr Clynes got up (I think he had been a

[1] What a change now!

miner himself) he spoke with such sincerity and passion that those who had come to scoff remained to pray.

During the six terms that I was in Cambridge the relations between British and Indian students were on the whole quite cordial, but in few cases did they ripen into real friendship. I say this not from my personal experience alone but from general observation as well. Many factors were responsible for this. The war undoubtedly had its effect. One could detect in the average Britisher a feeling of superiority beneath a veneer of *bon-homie* which was not agreeable to others. On our side, after the post-war events in India and particularly the tragedy at Amritsar, we could not but be sensitive (perhaps ultra-sensitive) with regard to our self-respect and national honour. It also pained us to find that among middle-class Englishmen there was a great deal of sympathy for General Dyer. It is probable that speaking generally the basis for a friendship between Britishers and Indians did not exist. We were politically more conscious and more sensitive than we had been before. Consequently friendship with an Indian presupposed sympathy, or at least toleration, for his political ideas. That was not always easy to find. Among the political parties only Labour expressed sympathy for Indian aspirations. It followed that there was greater possibility of friendship with Labourites or people having pro-Labour views and sentiments.

The above remarks are of a general nature, and must provide for exceptions. I myself made friends with people, students and non-students, holding conservative views regarding British politics, which continues till the present day in spite of all that I have been through. That was possible because they had sufficient toleration for my ideas. The intelligentsia of Great Britain has been passing through something like an intellectual revolution during the last decade, and specially during the last five years, and I daresay that that is reflected in the atmosphere of Cambridge, Oxford, London, and other places. The experience of today may not therefore tally with that of 1919 and 1920.

That I have not misjudged British mentality as I found it soon after the war can be demonstrated from one or two incidents. It is generally claimed that the average Briton has a sense of fair-play, a sportsmanlike spirit. During my time at Cambridge we Indians wanted more proof of it. The tennis champion for the year was an Indian student, Sunder Dass, who naturally got the blue. We expected that he would be called upon to captain the team in the inter-varsity matches. But in order to frustrate that, an old blue who had already gone down was sent for and made to stay on for another year. On paper it was alright. The senior blue had the priority in the matter of captaining the team, but everybody knew what had passed behind the scenes and there was silent resentment in the ranks of the Indian students.

Another instance. One day we saw a notice inviting applications from undergraduates for enlistment in the University Officers' Training Corps. Some of us went up and applied. We were told that the question would have to be referred to the higher authorities. After some time came the reply that the India Office objected to our enlisting in the O.T.C. The matter was brought before the Indian Majlis and it was decided to take the matter up with the Secretary of State for India, and Mr K. L. Gauba and I were authorised to interview him if necessary. The then Secretary, Mr E. S.

Montague, referred us to the Under-Secretary of State for India, the Earl of Lytton, who received us cordially and gave us a patient hearing. He assured us that the India Office had no objection at all and that the opposition came from the War Office. The War Office was informed that the enlistment of Indians in the O.T.C. would be resented by British students. Further, the War Office was afraid that since members of the O.T.C., when fully qualified, were entitled to commissions in the British Army, a difficult situation would arise if Indian students after qualifying in the O.T.C. demanded commissions in the British Army. Lord Lytton added that personally he thought it was inevitable that in future Indian officers should be in charge of mixed regiments, but the prejudice against Indians unfortunately persisted in certain circles and could not be ignored. We replied that in order to obviate the difficulty we were prepared to give an assurance that we would not ask for commissions in the British Army. We added that we were more interested in getting the training than in joining the army as a profession. On returning to Cambridge we again tackled the O.T.C. staff, and we were again told that the War Office was not objecting to the proposal but the India Office. Whatever the truth, no doubt that there was prejudice against Indians in certain British circles. As long as I was there, our demands were not met by the authorities and I daresay the position is the same today as it was seventeen years ago.

Indian students at Cambridge at that time had, on the whole, a satisfactory record, especially in the matter of studies. In sports, too, they did not do badly at all. We would only have liked to see them doing well in boating. Now that boating is becoming popular in

India, it is to be hoped that in future they will figure conspicuously in boating also.

The question is often raised as to whether it is desirable to send Indian students abroad and if so at what age. In 1920 an official Committee was appointed, presided over by Lord Lytton, to consider the affairs of Indian students in Great Britain, and this point was also discussed in connection therewith. My considered opinion was and still is that Indian students should go abroad only when they have attained a certain level of maturity. In other words, as a rule, they should go after graduation. In that case they can make the most of their stay abroad. This was the view that I put forward when I represented the Cambridge Indian Majlis before the above Indian Students' Committee. Much is made of public school-training in Britain. I do not desire to express any opinion as to how it affects British people and British students. But so far as Indian students are concerned, I do not have a kind word for it. At Cambridge I came across some Indian products of English public schools and I did not think highly of them.[1] Those who had their parents living with them in England and had home influence to supplement their school-education fared better than those who were quite alone. Education in the lower stages must be 'national,' it must have its roots in the soil. We must draw our mental pabulum from the culture of our own country. How can that be possible if one is transplanted at too early an age? No, we should not, as a rule, countenance the idea of sending boys and girls to schools abroad quite alone at an immature age. Education becomes international at the higher stages. It is then that students can, with profit, go abroad, and it is then that the

[1] Every rule has its exceptions, of course.

East and the West can commingle to the benefit of both.

In India members of the Civil Service used to be known formerly as 'subjunta', or one who knows everything. There was some justification for that because they used to be put up to all kinds of jobs. The education that they received did give them a certain amount of elasticity and a smattering of a large number of subjects which was helpful to them in actual administration. I realised this when I sat for the Civil Service Examination, with nine subjects on my shoulders. Not all of them have been useful to me in later life, but I must say that the study of Political Science, Economics, English History, and Modern European History proved to be beneficial. This was specially the case with Modern European History. Before I studied this subject I did not have a clear idea of the politics of Continental Europe. We Indians are taught to regard Europe as a magnified edition of Great Britain. Consequently we have a tendency to look at the Continent through the eyes of England. This is, of course, a gross mistake, but not having been to the Continent, I did not realise it till I studied Modern European History and some of its original sources like Bismarck's *Autobiography*, Metternich's *Memoirs*, Cavour's *Letters*, etc. These original sources, more than anything else, I studied at Cambridge, helped to rouse my political sense and to foster my understanding of the inner currents of international politics.

Early in July, 1920, the Civil Service open competitive examination began in London. It dragged on for a month and the agony was a prolonged one. I had worked hard, on the whole, but my preparation was far below my expectation. So I could not feel hopeful. So many brilliant students had come down in spite of years of preparation that it would require some conceit to feel anything but diffident. My diffidence was heightened when I foolishly threw away about 150 sure marks in my Sanskrit paper. It was the translation paper, English to Sanskrit, and I had done it well. I prepared a rough copy of the translation first with the intention of making a fair copy in the answer-book. But so oblivious was I of the time that when the bell went, I had transcribed only a portion of the text I had prepared in rough. But there was no help—the answer-book had to be surrendered and I could only bite my fingers.

I informed my people that I had not done well and could not hope to find a place among the selected candidates. I now planned to continue my work for the Tripos. Imagine my surprise, therefore, when I got a telegram one night when I was in London from a friend of mine which ran thus—"CONGRATULATIONS SEE MORNING POST." I wondered what it meant. Next morning when I got a copy of the *Morning Post*, I found that I had come out fourth. I was glad. A cable went off to India at once.

I had now another problem to face. What should I do with the job? Was I going to give the go-by to all my dreams and aspirations, and settle down to a comfortable life? There was nothing new in that. So many had done it before—so many had talked big when they were young and had acted differently when grown up. I knew of a young man from Calcutta who had Ramakrishna and Vivekananda at the tip of his tongue in his college days, but later on married into a rich family and was now safely landed in the Indian Civil Service. Then there was the case of a friend from Bombay who had promised in the presence of the late Lokamanya Tilak that, if he happened to pass the I.C.S. Examination, he would resign and devote himself to national work.[1] But I had resolved early in life not to follow the beaten track and, further, I had certain ideals which I wanted to live up to. It was therefore quite impossible for me to go into the Service unless I could make a clean sweep of my past life.

There were two important considerations which I had to weigh before I could think of resigning. Firstly, what would my people think? Secondly, if I resigned now in a fit of excitement, would I have any occasion in future to regret my action? Was I absolutely sure that I was doing the right thing?

It took me seven long months to make up my mind. In the meantime, I started a correspondence with my second brother, Sarat. Fortunately the letters I wrote have been preserved by him. The ones I received have

[1] When Lokamanya B. G. Tilak visited Cambridge in 1919 he appealed to the Indian students not to go in for Government service but to devote themselves to national service. He regretted that so many bright and promising students were hankering after Government jobs. This friend in a fit of inspiration stood up and announced that, though he was trying to qualify for the Indian Civil Service, if he managed to pass the examination, he would resign and then serve the national cause. He did not pass the first time but the next year he was successful and he is now in the service.

When Lokamanya Tilak was to visit Cambridge, the Indian Office and the Foreign Office became nervous. Lord Curzon, who was then the Foreign Secretary, wrote to the Vice-Chancellor requesting him to stop his visit if possible. The Vice-Chancellor sent for the Indian students in that connection, but they declared that since Lokamanya Tilak had already been invited, it was quite impossible to cancel his visit. Thereafter, there was no interference on the part of the University, Lord Curzon's letter notwithstanding.

The burden of Lokamanya Tilak's speech at Cambridge was that he demanded 'Home Rule within fifteen years.' Some English undergrads who had heard that Lokamanya Tilak was a firebrand came to the lecture expecting some hot stuff. After the lecture they remarked: "If these are your extremists, we don't want to hear your moderates."

all been lost in the storm and stress of a hectic political life. My letters are interesting inasmuch as they show the working of my mind in 1920.

The I.C.S. Examination result was declared about the middle of September, 1920. A few days later when I was taking a holiday at Leigh-on-Sea in Essex I wrote to him on the 22nd September as follows:—

"I was so glad to receive the telegram conveying congratulations. I don't know whether I have gained anything really substantial by passing the I.C.S. Examination—but it is a great pleasure to think that the news has pleased so many and especially that it has delighted father and mother in these dark days.

"I am here as a paying guest of Mr B.'s family. Mrs B. represents English character at its very best. He is cultured and liberal in his views and cosmopolitan in his sentiments . . . . Mr B. counts among his friends Russians, Poles, Lithuanians, Irishmen, and members of other nationalities. He takes a great interest in Russian, Irish and Indian literature, and admires the writings of Ramesh Dutt and Tagore . . . . I have been getting heaps of congratulations on my standing fourth in the competitive examination. But I cannot say that I am delighted at the prospect of entering the ranks of the I.C.S. If I have to join this service I shall do so with as much reluctance as I started my study for the C.S. Examination with. A nice flat income with a good pension in after-life—I shall surely get. Perhaps I may become a Commissioner if I stoop to make myself servile enough. Given talents, with a servile spirit one may even aspire to be the Chief Secretary to a provincial Government. But after all is Service to be the be-all and end-all of my life? The Civil Service can bring one all kinds of worldly comfort, but are not these acquisitions made at the expense of one's soul? I think it is hypocrisy to maintain that the highest ideals of one's life are compatible with subordination to the conditions of service which an I.C.S. man has got to accept.

"You will readily understand my mental condition as I stand on the threshold of what the man-in-the-street would call a promising career. There is much to be said in favour of such a service. It solves once for all what is the paramount problem for each of us—the problem of bread and butter. One has not to go to face life with risk or any uncertainty as to success or failure. But for a man of my temperament who has been feeding on ideas which might be called eccentric—the line of least resistance is not the best line to follow. Life loses half its interest if there is no struggle—if there are no risks to be taken. The uncertainties of life are not appalling to one who has not, at heart, worldly ambitions. Moreover, it is not possible to serve one's country in the best and fullest manner if one is chained to the Civil Service. In short, national and spiritual aspirations are not compatible with obedience to Civil Service conditions.

"I realise that it is needless to talk in this fashion as my will is not my own. Though I am sure that the C. Service has no glamour for you, father is sure to be hostile to the idea of my not joining. He would like to see me settled down in life as soon as possible. . . Hence I find that owing to sentimental and economic reasons, my will can hardly be called my own. But I may say without hesitation that if I were given the option—I would be the last man to join the Indian Civil Service.

"You may rightly say that, instead of avoiding the service, one should enter its ranks and fight its evils. But even if I do so, my position any day may become so intolerable as to compel me to resign. If such a crisis takes place 5 or 10 years hence, I shall not be in a favourable position to chalk out a new line for myself—whereas today there is yet time for me to qualify for another career.

"If one is cynical enough one may say that all this 'spirit' will evaporate as soon as I am safe in the arms of the service. But I am determined not to submit to that sickening influence. I am not going to marry—hence considerations of worldly prudence will not deter me from taking a particular line of action if I believe that to be intrinsically right.

"Constituted as I am, I have sincere doubts as to whether I should be a fit man for the Civil Service and I rather think that what little capacity I possess can be better utilised in other directions for my own welfare as well as for the welfare of my country.

"I should like to know your opinion about this. I have not written to father on this point—I really don't know why. I wish I could get his opinion too."

The above letter shows that the conflict had begun but was still far from being resolved. On the 26th January, 1921, I reverted to the subject and wrote :—

". . . . You may say that instead of shunning this wicked system we should enter it and fight with it till the last. But such a fight one has got to carry on single-handed in spite of censure from above, transfer to unhealthy places, and stoppage of promotion. The amount of good that one can do while in the service is infinitesimal when compared with what one can do when outside it. Mr R. C. Dutt no doubt did a lot of work in spite of his service but I am sure he could have done much more work if he had not been a member of the bureaucracy. Besides the question here involved is one of principle. On principle I cannot accept the idea of being a part of the machinery which has outlived the days of its usefulness, and stands at present for all that is connected with conservatism, selfish power, heartlessness, and red-tapism.

"I am now at the cross-ways and no compromise is possible. I must either chuck this rotten service and dedicate myself whole-heartedly to the country's cause —or I must bid adieu to all my ideals and aspirations and enter the service . . . . I am sure many of our relatives will howl when they hear of such a rash and dangerous proposal . . . . But I do not care for their opinions, their cheers or their taunts. But I have faith in your idealism and that is why I am appealing to you. About this time 5 years ago I had your moral support in an endeavour which was fraught with disastrous consequences to myself. For a year my future was dark and blank, but I bore the consequences bravely, I never complained to myself, and today I am proud that I had the strength to make that sacrifice. The memory of that event strengthens my belief that if any demands for sacrifice are made upon me in the future I shall respond with equal fortitude, courage and calmness. And in this new endeavour can I not expect the same moral support which you so willingly and so nobly lent me, five years ago? . . . .

"I am writing to father separately this time and am appealing to him to give his consent. I hope that if you agree with my point of view you will try to persuade father to that effect. I am sure your opinion in this matter will carry great weight."

This letter of the 26th January, 1921, shows that I had moved towards a decision but was still awaiting approval from home.

The next letter in which there was reference to the same topic was dated the 16th February, 1921. I wrote therein :—

". . . . You have received my 'explosive' letter by this time. Further thought confirms me in my support of the plans I have sketched for myself in that letter. . . . . If C. R. Das at his age can give up everything and face the uncertainties of life—I am sure a young man like myself, who has no worldly cares to trouble him, is much more capable of doing so. If I give up the service, I shall not be in want of work to keep my hands full. Teaching, social service, co-operative credit work, journalism, village organization work, these are so many things to keep thousands of energetic young men busy. Personally, I should like teaching and journalism at present. The National College and the new paper *Swaraj* will afford plenty of scope for my activity. . . . A life of sacrifice to start with, plain living and high thinking, whole-hearted devotion to the country's cause —all these are highly enchanting to my imagination and inclination. Further, the very principle of serving under an alien bureaucracy is intensely repugnant to me. The path of Arabindo Ghosh is to me more noble, more inspiring, more lofty, more unselfish, though more thorny than the patch of Ramesh Dutt.

"I have written to father and to mother to permit me to take the vow of poverty and service. They may be frightened at the thought that that path might lead to suffering in the future. Personally I am not afraid of suffering—in fact, I would rather welcome it than shrink from it."

The letter of the 23rd February, 1921, is also interesting. Therein I say :—

"Ever since the result of the I.C.S. was declared, I have been asking myself whether I shall be more useful to my country if I am in the service than if I am not. I am fully convinced now that I shall be able to serve my country better if I am one of the people than if I am a member of the bureaucracy. I do not deny that one can do some amount of good when he is in the service but it can't be compared with the amount of good that one can do when his hands are not tied by bureaucratic chains. Besides, as I have already mentioned in one of my letters, the question involved is mainly one of principle. The principle of serving an alien bureaucracy is one to which I cannot reconcile myself. Besides the first step towards equipping oneself for public service is to sacrifice all worldly interests—to burn one's boats as it were—and devote oneself wholeheartedly to the national cause. . . . . The illustrious example of Arabindo Ghosh looms large before my vision. I feel that I am ready to make the sacrifice which that example demands of me. My circumstances are also favourable."

It is clear from the above that I was still under the influence of Arabindo Ghosh. As a matter of fact it was widely believed about this time that he would soon return to active political life.

The next letter was written on the 6th April from Oxford where I was spending my holidays. By then I had received my father's letter disapproving of my plans, but I had definitely made up my mind to resign. The following extracts are interesting :—

"Father thinks that the life of a self-respecting Indian Civil Servant will not be intolerable under the new regime and that home rule will come to us within ten years. But to me the question is not whether my life will be tolerable under the new regime. In fact, I believe that, even if I am in the service, I can do some useful work. The main question involved is one of principle. Should we under the present circumstances own allegiance to a foreign bureaucracy and sell ourselves for a mess of pottage? Those who are already in the service or who cannot help accepting service may do so. But should I, being favourably situated in many respects, own allegiance so readily? The day I sign the covenant I shall cease to be a free man.

"I believe we shall get Home Rule within ten years and certainly earlier if we are ready to pay the price. The price consists of sacrifice and suffering. Only on the soil of sacrifice and suffering can we raise our national edifice. If we all stick to our jobs and look after our own interests, I don't think we shall get Home Rule even in 50 years. Each family—if not each individual—should now bring forward its offering to the feet of the mother. Father wants to save me from this sacrifice. I am not so callous as not to appreciate the love and affection which impels him to save me from this sacrifice, in my own interests. He is naturally apprehensive that I am perhaps hasty in my judgement or overzealous in my youthful enthusiasm. But I am perfectly convinced that the sacrifice has got to be made—by somebody at least.

"If anybody else had come forward, I might have had cause to withdraw or wait. Unfortunately nobody is coming yet and the precious moments are flying away. In spite of all the agitation going on there, it still remains true that not a single Civil Servant has had the courage to throw away his job and join the people's movement. This challenge has been thrown at India and has not been answered yet. I may go further and say that in the whole history of British India, not one Indian has voluntarily given up the Civil Service with a patriotic motive. It is time that members of the highest service in India should set an example to members of the other services. If the members of the services withdraw their allegiance or even show a desire to do so—then only will the bureaucratic machine collapse.

"I therefore do not see how I can save myself from this sacrifice. I know what this sacrifice means. It means poverty, suffering, hard work, and possibly other hardships to which I need not expressly refer, but which you can very well understand. But the sacrifice has got to be made—consciously and deliberately. . . . Your proposal that I should resign after returning is eminently reasonable but there are one or two points to be urged against it. In the first place it will be a galling thing for me to sign the covenant which is an emblem of servitude. In the second place if I accept service for the present I shall not be able to return home before December or January, as the usual custom stands. If I resign now, I may return by July. In six months' time much water will have flowed through the Ganges. In the absence of adequate response at the right moment, the whole movement might tend to flag, and if response comes too late it may not have any effect. I believe it will take years to initiate another such movement and hence I think that the tide in the present movement must be availed of. If I have to resign, it does not make any difference to me or to any one of us whether I resign tomorrow or after a year, but delay in resigning may on the other hand have some untoward effect on the movement. I know full well that I can do but little to help the movement—but it will be a great thing if I have the satisfaction of having done my bit. . . . . If for any reason I happen to change my decision regarding resignation, I shall send a cable to father as that will relieve his anxiety."

In the letter written from Cambridge on the 20th April, I said that I would send in my resignation on the 22nd April.

In my letter dated the 28th April from Cambridge I wrote as follows :—

"I had a talk with the Censor of Fitzwilliam Hall, Mr Reddaway, about my resignation. Contrary to my expectations, he heartily approved of my ideas. He said he was surprised, almost shocked, to hear that I had changed my mind, since no Indian within his knowledge had ever done that before. I told him that I would make journalism my profession later on, and he said that he preferred a journalistic career to a monotonous one like the Civil Service.

"I was at Oxford for three weeks before I came up here and there the final stage of my deliberation took place. The only point which had been taxing me for the last few months was whether I should be justified morally in following a course which would cause intense sorrow and displeasure in many minds and especially in the minds of father and mother. . . . My position therefore is that, in entering a new career, I am acting against the express wishes of father and mother and against your advice though you have sent me your 'warmest felicitations in whatever course I choose.' My greatest objection to joining the service was based on the fact that I would have to sign the covenant and thereby own the allegiance of a foreign bureaucracy which I feel rightly or wrongly has no moral right to be there. Once I signed the covenant, it would not matter from the point of view of principle whether I served for three days or three years. I have come to believe that compromise is a bad thing—it degrades the man and injures his cause. . . . The reason why Surendra Nath Bannerji is going to end his life with a knighthood and a ministership is that he is a worshipper of the philosophy of expediency which Edmund Burke preached. We have not come to that stage where we can accept a philosophy of expediency. We have got to make a nation and a nation can be made only by the uncompromising idealism of Hampden and Cromwell. . . . . I have come to believe that it is time for us to wash our hands clean of any connection with the British Government. Every Government servant whether he be a petty chaprasi or a provincial Governor only helps to contribute to the stability of the British Government in India. The best way to end a Government is to withdraw from it. I say this not because that that was Tolstoy's doctrine nor because Gandhi preaches it—but because I have come to believe in it. . . . I sent in my resignation a few days ago. I have not yet been informed that it has been accepted.

"C. R. Das has written, in reply to a letter of mine, about the work that is already being done. He complains that there is a dearth of sincere workers at present. There will consequently be plenty of congenial work for me when I return home. . . . I have nothing more to say. The die is cast and I earnestly hope that nothing but good will come out of it."

On the 18th May, I wrote from Cambridge as follows:—

"Sir William Duke is trying to persuade me to withdraw my resignation. He wrote to Bardada about it.

The Secretary of the Civil Service Board at Cambridge, Mr Roberts, also asked me to reconsider my decision and he said he was acting under instruction from the India Office. I have sent word to Sir William saying that I have acted after mature deliberation."

This letter requires an annotation. Soon after I sent in my resignation, there was a flutter in the India Office dovecots. The late Sir William Duke, then Permanent Under-Secretary of State for India, who knew my father when he was Commissioner of Orissa, got into touch with my eldest brother, Sjt Satish Chandra Bose, who was then qualifying himself for the Bar in London. Sir William advised me through my brother not to resign the service. I was also approached by lecturers in Cambridge and asked to reconsider my decision. Then there was a request from the Secretary of the Civil Service Board in Cambridge, the late Mr Roberts. All these moves taken from different directions intrigued me, but most interesting of all was the last move.

Some months earlier I had a passage-at-arms with Mr Roberts over some printed instructions issued to Civil Service Probationers by the India Office. These instructions were under the caption "Care of Horses in India" and contained remarks to the effect that the India syce (groom) eats the same food as his horse—that Indian Bunnias (traders) are proverbially dishonest, etc. I naturally felt indignant when I received them and had a talk with other fellow-probationers who had also got them. We all agreed that the instructions were incorrect and offensive and that we should make a joint protest. When the time came for us to write, everybody tried to back out. Ultimately I grew desperate and decided to act on my own . . . .

CHAPTER TEN

MY FAITH (PHILOSOPHICAL)

In 1917 I became very friendly with a Jesuit father. We used to have long talks on matters of common interest. In the Jesuit order founded by Ignatius Loyala I then found much that appealed to me, for instance, their triple vow of poverty, chastity, and obedience.[1] Unlike many Jesuits, this father was not dogmatic and he was well versed in Hindu philosophy. In our discussions he naturally took his stand on Christian theology as interpreted by his church, while I took my stand on the Vedanta as interpreted by Shankaracharya. I did not of course comprehend the Shankarite Doctrine of Maya[2] in all its abstruseness, but I grasped the essential principles of it—or at least I thought I did. One day the Jesuit father turned round to me and said—"I admit that Shankara's position is logically the soundest—but to those who cannot live up to it, we offer the next best."

There was a time when I believed that Absolute Truth was within the reach of human mind and that the Doctrine of Maya represented the quintessence of knowledge. Today I would hesitate to subscribe to that position. I have ceased to be an absolutist (if I may use that word in my own sense) and am much more of a pragmatist. What I cannot live up to—what is not

[1] There is some analogy to the triple prayer of the Buddhists which has to be repeated daily—"I take refuge in Buddha; I take refuge in Dharma (Truth); I take refuge in the Sangha (Order)."

[2] In brief, this theory implies that the world as we perceive it through our senses is an illusion. It is a case of the rope being mistaken for a snake, the snake being the world of the senses.

workable—I feel inclined to discard. Shankara's Doctrine of Maya intrigued me for a long time, but ultimately I found that I could not accept it because I could not live it. So I had to turn to a different philosophy. But that did not oblige me to go to Christian theology. There are several schools of Indian philosophy which regard the world, creation, as a reality and not as an illusion. There is, for example, the theory of Qualified monism according to which the ultimate reality is One and the world is a manifestation of it. Ramakrishna's view is similar, that both the One (God) and the Many (Creation) are true. Several theories have been advanced to explain the nature of creation. According to some the universe is the manifestation of Ananda or Divine Bliss. Others hold that it is the manifestation of Divine Play or 'Leela'. Several attempts have also been made to describe the One—the Absolute—God—in human language and imagery. To some, like the Vaishnavas, God is Love; to some like the Shaktas, He is Power; to others He is Knowledge; to still others He is Bliss. Then there is the traditional conception of the Absolute in Hindu philosophy as 'Sat-Chit-Ananda', which may be translated as 'Existence-Consciousness (or Knowledge)-Bliss'. The more consistent philosophers say that the Absolute is indescribable or inexpressible (anirvachaneeya). And it is reported of Buddha that whenever he was questioned about the Absolute he remained silent.

It is impossible to comprehend the Absolute through our human intellect with all its limitations. We cannot perceive reality as it is objectively—as it is in itself—we have to do so through our own spectacles, whether these spectacles be Bacon's 'Idola' or Kant's 'forms of the understanding' or something else. The Hindu philosopher will probably say that as long as the duality of Subject (Jnata) and Object (Jneya) remains, knowledge is bound to be imperfect. Perfect knowledge can be attained only when Subject and Object merge into oneness. This is not possible on the mental plane—the plane of ordinary consciousness. It is possible only in the supra-mental plane—in the region of superconsciousness. But the conception of the supra-mental, of the super-conscious, is peculiar to Hindu philosophy and is repudiated by Western philosophers. According to the former, perfect knowledge is attainable only when we reach the level of the super-conscious through Yogic perception, i.e., intuition of some sort. Intuition as an instrument of knowledge has, of course, been admitted in Western philosophy since the time of Henri Bergson, though it may still be ridiculed in certain quarters. But Western philosophy has yet to admit the existence of the supra-mental and the possibility of our comprehending it through Yogic perception.

Assuming for a moment for argument's sake that we can comprehend the Absolute through Yogic perception, the difficulty about describing it will still remain. When we attempt to describe it, we fall back into the plane of normal consciousness and we are handicapped by all the limitations of the normal human mind. Our descriptions of the Absolute of God are consequently anthropomorphic. And what is anthropomorphic cannot be regarded as Absolute Truth.

Now can we comprehend the Absolute through Yogic perception? Is there a supra-mental plane which the individual can reach and where the Subject and the Object merge into Oneness? My attitude to this question is one of benevolent agnosticism—if I may coin this expression. On the one hand, I am not prepared to take anything on trust. I must have first-hand experience, but this sort of experience in the matter of the Absolute, I am unable to get. On the other hand, I cannot just rule out as sheer moonshine what so many individuals claim to have experienced in the past. To repudiate all that would be to repudiate much, which I am not prepared to do. I have, therefore, to leave the question of the supra-mental open, until such time as I am able to experience it myself. Meanwhile I take up the position of a relativist. I mean thereby, that Truth as known to us is not absolute but relative. It is relative to our common mental constitution—to our distinctive characteristics as individuals—and to changes in the same individual during the process of time.

Once we admit that our notions of the Absolute are relative to our human mind, we should be relieved of a great deal of philosophical controversy. It would follow that when such notions differ, they may all be equally true—the divergence being accounted for by the distinctive individuality of the subject. It would follow, further, that the notions of the same individual with regard to the Absolute may vary with time along with his mental development. But none of these notions need be regarded as false. As Vivekananda used to say, "Man proceeds not from error to truth but from truth to higher truth." There should accordingly be scope for the widest toleration.

The question now arises: Granting that reality as known to me is relative and not absolute, what is its nature? In the first place, it has an objective existence and is not an illusion. I come to this conclusion not from *a priori* considerations but mainly from the pragmatic point of view. The Doctrine of Maya does not work. My life is incompatible with it, though I tried long and hard to make my life fit in with it. I have, therefore, to discard it. On the other hand, if the world be real (not, of course, in an absolute but in a relative sense) then life becomes interesting and acquires meaning and purpose.

Secondly, this reality is not static—but dynamic—it is ever changing. Has this change any direction? Yes, it has; it is moving towards a better state of existence. Actual experience demonstrates that the changes imply progress—and not meaningless motion.

Further, this reality is, for me, Spirit working with a conscious purpose through time and space. This conception does not, of course, represent the Absolute Truth which is beyond description for all time and which for me is also beyond comprehension at the present moment. It is therefore a relative truth and is liable to change along with the changes in my mind.[1] Nevertheless, it is a conception which represents my utmost effort to comprehend reality and which offers a basis on which to build my life.

Why do I believe in Spirit? Because it is a pragmatic necessity. My nature demands it. I see purpose and design in nature; I discern an 'increasing purpose' in my own life. I feel that I am not a mere conglomeration of atoms. I perceive, too, that reality is not a fortuitous combination of molecules. Moreover, no other theory can explain reality (as I understand it) so well. This theory is in short an intellectual and moral necessity, a necessity of my very life, so far as I am concerned.

[1] There is nothing wrong in this—for, as Emerson said, a foolish consistency is the hobgoblin of little minds. Moreover, what is progress if it does not involve change?

The world is a manifestation of Spirit and just as Spirit is eternal so also is the world of creation. Creation does not and cannot end at any point of time. This view is similar to the Vaishnavic conception of Eternal Play (Nitya Leela). Creation is not the offspring of sin; nor is it the result of 'avidya' or 'ignorance' as the Shankarites would say. It reflects the eternal play of eternal forces—the Divine Play, if you will.

I may very well be asked why I am bothering about the ultimate nature of reality and similar problems and am not contenting myself with experience as I find it. The answer to that is simple. The moment we analyse experience, we have to posit the self—the mind which receives—and the non-self—the source of all impressions, which form the stuff of our experience. The non-self—reality apart from the self—is there and we cannot ignore its existence by shutting our eyes to it. This reality underlies all our experience and on our conception of it depends much that is of theoretical and practical value to us.

No, we cannot ignore reality. We must endeavour to know its nature—though, as I have already indicated, that knowledge can at best be relative and cannot be dignified with the name of Absolute Truth. This relative truth must form the basis of our life—even if what is relative is liable to change.

What then is the nature of this Spirit which is reality? One is reminded of the parable of Ramakrishna about a number of blind men trying to describe an elephant—each giving a description in accordance with the organ he touched and therefore violently disagreeing with the rest. My own view is that most of the conceptions of reality are true, though partially, and the main question is which conception represents the maximum truth. For me, the essential nature of reality is LOVE. LOVE is the essence of the Universe and is the essential principle in human life. I admit that this conception also is imperfect—for I do not know today what reality is in itself and I cannot lay claim to knowing the Absolute today—even if it be within the ultimate reach of human knowledge or experience. Nevertheless, with all its imperfection, for me this theory represents the maximum truth and is the nearest approach to Absolute Truth.

I may be asked how I come to the conclusion that the essential nature of reality is LOVE. I am afraid my epistemology is not quite orthodox. I have come to this conclusion partly from a rational study of life in all aspects—partly from intuition and partly from pragmatic considerations. I see all around me the play of love; I perceive within me the same instinct; I feel that I must love in order to fulfil myself and I need love as the basic principle on which to reconstruct life. A plurality of considerations drives me to one and the same conclusion.

I have remarked above that the essential principle in human life is love. This statement may be challenged when one can see so much in life that is opposed to love; but the paradox can be easily explained. The 'essential principle' is not fully manifest yet; it is unfolding itself in space and time. Love, like reality of which it is the essence, is dynamic.

What, now, is the nature of the process of unfolding? Firstly, is it a movement forward or not? Secondly, is there any law underlying this movement?

The unfolding process is progressive in character. This assertion is not quite dogmatic. Observation and study of nature point to the conclusion that everywhere there is progress. This progress may not be unilinear; there may be periodic set-backs—but on the whole, i.e. considered from a long period point of view, there is progress. Apart from this rational consideration there is the intuitive experience that we are moving ahead with the lapse of time. And last but not least, there is the necessity, both biological and moral, to have faith in progress.

As various attempts have been made to know reality and to describe it—so also have attempts been made to comprehend the law of progress. None of these efforts is futile; each gives us a glimpse of the truth. The Sankhya Philosophy of the Hindus was probably the oldest endeavour to describe the evolutionary process in nature. That solution will not satisfy the modern mind. In more recent times, we have various theories, or perhaps descriptions, of evolution. Some like Spencer would have us believe that evolution consists in a development from the simple to the complex. Others like von Hartmann would assert that the world is a manifestation of blind will—from which one could conclude that it is futile to look for an underlying idea. Bergson would maintain his own theory of creative evolution; evolution should imply a new creation or departure at every stage, which cannot be calculated in advance by the human intellect. Hegel, on the contrary, would dogmatise that the nature of the evolutionary process, whether in the thought world or in reality outside, is dialectic. We progress through conflicts and their solutions. Every thesis provokes an antithesis. This conflict is solved by a synthesis, which in its turn, provokes a new antithesis—and so on.

All these theories have undoubtedly an element of truth. Each of the above thinkers has endeavoured to reveal the truth as he has perceived it. But undoubtedly Hegel's theory is the nearest approximation to truth. It explains the facts more satisfactorily than any other theory. At the same time, it cannot be regarded as the whole truth since all the facts as we know them, do not accord with it. Reality is, after all, too big for our frail understanding to fully comprehend. Nevertheless, we have to build our life on the theory which contains the maximum truth. We cannot sit still because we cannot, or do not, know the Absolute Truth.

Reality, therefore, is Spirit, the essence of which is Love, gradually unfolding itself in an eternal play of conflicting forces and their solutions.